Celebrating life is My Religion

JOAN'S JOURNEY THROUGH ABUSE, GRIEF, JOY, AND SURVIVAL

TERESKA E. JAMES

IN MEMORY OF TANYA,

AND FOR GRAYSON AND DE'ANDRE WHO'VE HAD

A FRONT ROW SEAT TO CELEBRATING LIFE WITH THEIR

G-MAMA SINCE THEY WERE BORN.

JOAN WITH HER G-BABIES DE'ANDRE AND GRAYSON.

Copyright © 2024 by Tereska E. James
ISBN: 979-8-218-49437-7 (paperback)
ISBN: 979-8-218-49930-3 (digital)

This book is a memoir. It reflects the author's present recollection of experiences over time. To protect the privacy of certain individuals, some names and characteristics have been changed, some events have been compressed, and some dialogue has been recreated.

Cover & Interior Design by Coco Anderson
Cover Photography by So Focused Photography
Author Photo by Justin Clynes Studio
Edited by Shawn Haugen and Stacey Small

WWW.TRESSIEANDNANA.COM

CONTENTS

FOWARD	VII
PROLOGUE	XII
STARTED FROM THE BOTTOM	17
GROWING PAINS	24
NO FEAR	30
SOME HEROES DON'T WEAR CAPES	33
WE ARE FAMILY	37
OH, BABY	45
THE MEN	53
THE FAMILY AFFAIR	78
WE ALL GOT RELIGION	85
JOAN'S HOUSE	89
WORKING GIRL	98
DAILY MEDICINE	103
DIDN'T SEE THAT COMING	108
AFTERWORD	115

FORWARD

During the summer of 2022, I set out to celebrate my mother's 70th birthday in a unique way. It all started on June 4th with this message that I posted on Facebook:

> "The more you praise and celebrate your life, the more there is in life to celebrate." — Oprah Winfrey
>
> As we journey through life's daily trials where we are navigating grief and tragedy...(especially in these past few years and even weeks or days), we have to give ourselves permission to also hold space for life's joys in whatever way we find (e.g., listening to your favorite song, dancing, working in your garden, eating a scoop of ice cream, etc.).
>
> It's necessary to our survival and mental health.
>
> As many of you know, this August marks my mom my Joan's (aka G-Mama) 70th Birthday.
>
> And, in honor of her life's motto to "Celebrate Life" which she does every day, I am doing a 70 to 70 countdown to August 14th starting tomorrow June 5th, to celebrate her in a special way + to show her that... yes, I've been listening and watching all these years.
>
> I invite you to join me!
>
> Here's how:
>
> Find the simple joy in everyday by celebrating

> life...feel free to post on your own page with the hashtags #celebratelifewithjoan
>
> #70DaysofJoan and tag me @tereskajames and my mom @joangmitchell
>
> AND/OR
>
> Add what you're doing in the comment section on my daily posts starting on Sunday, June 5th.
>
> Looking forward to celebrating life with you!

Each day without fail...70 days leading up to my mother's birthday, I posted or had a guest poster. After receiving an overwhelming response to the stories I shared and having a huge number of people tell me that I should write a book — and since my mom had asked me for years to write her life story, I decided to do it. After countless hours of interviews and note taking, this book represents my fulfillment of the promise I made to my mom on her 70th birthday. I've also included select social media posts from that time to accompany my mom's telling of her story.

My wish is that this book offers motivation, hope and insight into the woman who continues to be my daily inspiration and champion.

FORWARD

JOAN CELEBRATING LIFE IN THE BAHAMAS.

CELEBRATING LIFE IS MY RELIGION

THE 70 TO 70 PROJECT

The impetus for this 70 to 70 "project" derived from when I did a 40 to 40 journey years ago leading up to my 40th birthday where I posted every day about things I was doing to celebrate my milestone birthday.

Since this is a milestone birthday for my mom and I knew she didn't want any more huge parties, I thought this would be a good way to celebrate her, her life's motto and to share with friends and family.

My intention was to spread some joy, inspiration, and love. I didn't think much about "likes" or who was reading.

I will say that I've been extremely touched by your comments and messages received on and off social media. I love seeing the excitement on my mom's face and hearing it in her voice after she's read the posts each morning. Each post has been a fresh reveal to her... she finds out at the same time you do. I call or send her a text that the post is up. She's also been sharing them offline with her friends who aren't on social media.

I've always loved writing (and reading) ever since I was a little girl. For YEARS...like over 20+, my mom has literally begged me to write her memoir and every time I said "no, it's not my story to tell, it's yours, you write it". Then she would say "you're the writer, please Tress" and I'd still say "no." I even gave her a journal to start writing in and nada.

Toni Morrison said "If there's a book that you want to read,

FORWARD

but it hasn't been written yet, then you must write it."

So today, I'm saying "yes" to my mom and finally writing the book so many of you have said you want to read. I do too as I think I've only scratched the surface, even though I already know a lot about my mom. Happy Birthday Eve Mommy!

Side Note: This is not the book I thought I'd be writing, but it's the one calling me to write it now.

For years (too many to count or care to admit), I've been working on a fiction novel. In 2020 I declared, "this is the year" I'm going to finish! I shared my work in progress with a select few, but at a time that was so inspiring for many during the pandemic, I lost my writing mojo. I mentioned how I was feeling to my writing coach and she wrote back the following, "You have a gift of writing and it won't leave you. Your job is to nurture it. To bring it to its fullest potential. When the time is right you will write." I often reflect on these words and treasure them so very much.

While this 70-day journey was for my mom, it has done more for me than you'll ever know. Thank you again for following along.

Tomorrow is the BIG DAY.

#celebratelifewithjoan #70DaysofJoan

PROLOGUE

We delight in the beauty of the butterfly, but rarely admit the changes it has gone through to achieve that beauty.

MAYA ANGELOU

"I don't know how you're going to celebrate life now?" Those were words from an actual text message that someone sent me after the death of my daughter Tanya in 2015. I was surprised and shocked that they would say that...it was less than a month after she had passed. I was truly heartbroken and didn't know what I was going to do. I missed my daughter Tanya terribly and was hurt. I would have died for her...it didn't seem fair. She was so sweet and nice. I know people say crazy things when someone dies because they simply don't know what to say.

There was a time in my life where those words would have sent me spiraling into a state of worry and self-doubt...questioning and diving deeper into the intent of what the sender was really trying to say. I used to worry about what people thought and said about me for so long. It wasn't the first time someone made a remark about my positive attitude. In 1977 while I was working at IBM, I was stopped in the hallway by a man whose name I don't recall, but his words stuck with me. We had never spoken before that day and would only see each other in passing. He told me that I always seemed happy, like I didn't have a care in the world. He asked me what my

PROLOGUE

TANYA'S GRADUATION FROM DELAWARE STATE UNIVERSITY, 1995.

secret was, but at the time, I wasn't able to truly convey the "why" and "how" he wanted to know, I was consumed with insecurity and hiding behind my mask. These days, it's called imposter syndrome.

People didn't have a clue about what was going on in my life. It's only been in the past 10 years that I've come into myself. Other people's opinions of me have nothing to do with me and at 70, I could not care any less. Was asking how I would celebrate life now a snide remark, a test of my will, or as some would venture to say, "the work of the enemy?" I'd question whether I did indeed want—or even have the right—to celebrate. After all, I had just experienced one of the most, if not the most heart-wrenching and devastating things that I've been through in my life. The pain of losing a child is unmeasurable and doesn't seem to align with the universe and how we imagine the course of life to take shape. The young bury the old, not vice-versa.

Instead of meeting the question from a well-meaning friend negatively, I looked inward and received it with love. Yes, "how was I going to celebrate life now?" was not so much a question for me, but an awakening call to celebrate life even more. In the years since my daughter's passing, I've faced other challenges that would continue to reinforce the urgency of living in my truth and living my motto every day. Who I am today is vastly different from the shy, insecure, boney girl with the two broken front teeth from Townsend, Delaware.

My name is Joan Geraldine Mitchell. I was bestowed the name Joan by my brother Oscar. He had a lady friend who he said was very pretty and asked my mom if he could give me my first name. I have no clue where Geraldine originated.

The journey that I will share with you in these pages is a love letter to little Joan and all the girls, women, and people who are seeking a way to celebrate life in the midst of grief, heartbreak, sorrow, trauma, hardship, or anything that has you questioning "how do I celebrate life now?"

"Started from the bottom, now we're here...". Those are the words that caught my attention as I was partially trying to drown out the latest rap tune that was playing on the local R&B station as I drove down the highway a few years ago. I chuckled and began bopping along to the catchy lyrics and beat. I try to stay hip and keep an open mind, so my ears perked up and I gave into the rhythm. The

PROLOGUE

radio DJ said that the 2012 song by the famous Canadian rapper Drake was critically acclaimed and at the time was one of his best songs. When Drake released the track, he wrote a message on his website about how people didn't know enough about his beginnings and as a result, made up a life story for him that wasn't consistent with actual events. The thing that stuck most in my mind and what I reflected on was how those seven words took on a whole different meaning for me because I literally did start from the bottom and throughout my journey, people have counted me out and at times didn't want to see me thrive or celebrate life.

To those people, I only say thank you. Amazing

STARTED FROM THE BOTTOM

Celebrating the ones who made my mommy...my mom-mom and pop-pop Raleigh Lint Mitchell, 2/2/1912–6/18/1993 & Essamond Turner Mitchell, 12/27/1912–7/19/1997, may they continue to rest in heavenly peace.

There's so much that I could say about these two God-fearing souls, but the one thing I will say is that I'm grateful to have had the opportunity to grow up with my grandparents and experience daily life with them from the time I entered high school until I went to college, thanks to my mom. Three generations living under one roof with only one bathroom was not for the faint of heart. My aunts Barbara, Liz and Beulah and uncle Gene would probably call me a lightweight...oh, the stories I could tell.

If you're fortunate to still have your grandparents around, love on them today, and for those whose grandparents have gone on, do something to celebrate their memory today.

JOAN'S PARENTS, ESSAMOND AND RALEIGH MITCHELL.

STARTED FROM THE BOTTOM

[handwritten: Tell me about Joan's family home in Townsend, Delaware]

I don't remember too much before my family moved into our house in Townsend, Delaware as I was only about two or three years old. It wasn't actually a house, but started as a simple hole in the ground. My mother Essamond gave my father Raleigh the idea to lay the foundation for a house on the land that was purchased from a small inheritance she received from her father. The plan was to build out the basement for the family to live in while the actual house was under construction. Brilliant and novel idea because that way, our parents could save money and take time to build the main story of the dwelling, which was to be a three bedroom ranch style house with an attic and garage (which is still standing to this day). It became home for me and a safe haven full of pleasant and not so pleasant memories. The hole in the ground was a square, concrete box covered only by a flat wood surface and protected with tar to keep the water from entering the space. It contained a narrow, single-pane window we could barely see out of and a cellar door with steps that lead down to our cramped living quarters.

The basement was always dim as we didn't have electricity. Mom purchased what was called a piano floor lamp, which was fueled by kerosene. It was our main source of light along with a smaller, equally dim lamp that we'd have to take from room to room for any source of light. Our home was sectioned off by scant wood partitions and exposed ceiling beams. One area was where Mom and Daddy slept and another room had a makeshift bed for us kids, a main living area which was sparsely furnished with a small couch, a few chairs along with a cross and mirror for decorations. I don't recall whether the hard, dull gray concrete floors had at least a throw rug, but I imagine that wasn't a necessity. The final room was the kitchen which held our wood stove where our mom cooked our meals. It also served as a main source of heat in the cold, damp space. In the evening for entertainment, we either listened to Amos 'n' Andy on a battery-operated radio or old records on a phonograph.

Daddy liked to listen to the fights on the radio. It was one of the few times we saw him so animated as he cheered on his favorite boxer. Sundays consisted of church, which was non-negotiable in our household. We kneeled on the concrete floor and prayed in our pseudo "living room" both morning and evening, and spent Sunday afternoons and Wednesday and Friday nights at Little Mt. Olive Holiness Church in Smyrna, DE. Daddy was a Pentecostal minister and Mom was well-respected and made a head mother of the church later in life which was a title bestowed upon her by the pastor.

I do recall the basement flooding a lot and me being carried up the stairs. I also remember always being cold. Our home was never a warm place, especially during the winter. The warmth from the wood stove didn't reach our bedroom, so at night, Mom would place coats and homemade quilts on our bed from our aunt Lula. Her placing those extra layers was her unspoken way of showing love and care.

The silver lining to the space being so cold was that Mom was able to store our perishables under the stairs since it was the coolest area in the basement. We never seemed to have enough food, so not having an ice box wasn't an inconvenience. Mom made do with vegetables from her garden and eggs from the few hens we owned. Our diet consisted of lots of beans, greens, cream of wheat and hoe cakes. For flavor we used cheap butter called oleo and molasses.

Daddy raised hogs and chickens, so we'd have side meat to go with meals. We made do and mom was full of ingenuity. Always coming up with ways to skimp and save money. Once a month, we'd get a bag of penny candy and a soda as a treat. My favorites were mint julep, mary janes, squirrels, and a grape soda. I can still taste the sweetness on my tongue. Being able to go to the store in Blackbird, which was less than a mile from us, and charge it to our bill, was one of the highlights of my childhood. We didn't get many luxuries and to me, this was the main one.

We also didn't have indoor plumbing. Our outhouse was set off in the backyard away from the house. At night, a bucket was placed in the kids' room for us to do our business and Daddy would empty it in the morning. During the day, we sprinkled lime around the outhouse to keep the odor down. It still smelled awful, especially in the sweltering summer heat.

JOAN'S CHILDHOOD HOME IN TOWNSEND, DE.

Daddy would pump water from the outside well for us to use. We bathed once a week on Sunday. Mom would boil the water and fill a large metal tin for all five kids to bathe in, starting from the oldest (Elizabeth) to the youngest (Barbara). For the remainder of the week, our hygiene maintenance left a lot to be desired as we only washed the essential parts of the body. Pumping water from the well, bringing it into the house and heating it up on the wood stove took a lot of effort for Mom; this was her way of conserving water. Mom also used the same metal tin to wash our clothes. She'd use a mixture of Tide soap powder and bleach which was so strong, it made her hands raw and sore.

We were very poor and although many of our peers and their families were also poor, we soon realized that there were levels of poverty—and we were on the bottom rung.

Daddy worked on building the top portion of our home with a few Amish laborers after he got off work and during the weekends. Mom would often get rabbits from the Amish as a source of food. For a time, we were able to keep one or two as pets, but they always ended up on our plate, so we couldn't get too attached, it was food to us and Mom was more concerned with us being fed.

We finally moved from the basement to the main level when I was six. Our underground living situation, although temporary, set the stage for relentless bullying and teasing that my siblings and I received throughout our childhood, even from family. My sister, Barbara, was the only one who had been born while we were living in the basement, and people used to say…"Barbara, born in a hole where it was cold." We had a roof over our head, but we were still poor. I was always a sickly child. No one could ever figure out what was wrong with me. To this day, I believe it's what stunted my growth, as my siblings are all close to six feet or taller. I'm the short one of the bunch…so much so that there was a rumor going around that my mom had "relations" with another man and had me as a result.

What foolishness! Also adding to the rumor mill as recounted by two of my older siblings was the fact that I was very pretty and had soft, curly hair like a baby doll. I have no recollection or photos of myself or my siblings from when we were babies or young children, hence my obsession with taking pictures, but more on that later. The doctor came to our house a few times because my parents didn't think I'd survive. Having a doctor to make a house call or going to any doctor was a serious matter. Mom relied mainly on prayer and home remedies such as grated potatoes to kill a fever, castor oil and turpentine for colds, sassafras tea for stomach issues, and nutmeg paste with flour for diarrhea.

POST 65 OF 70

GROWING PAINS

Happy Monday!

Remember I told you that the only childhood picture my mom had of herself was from when she was in the 2nd grade...well, this is it and that's me in the 1st grade:

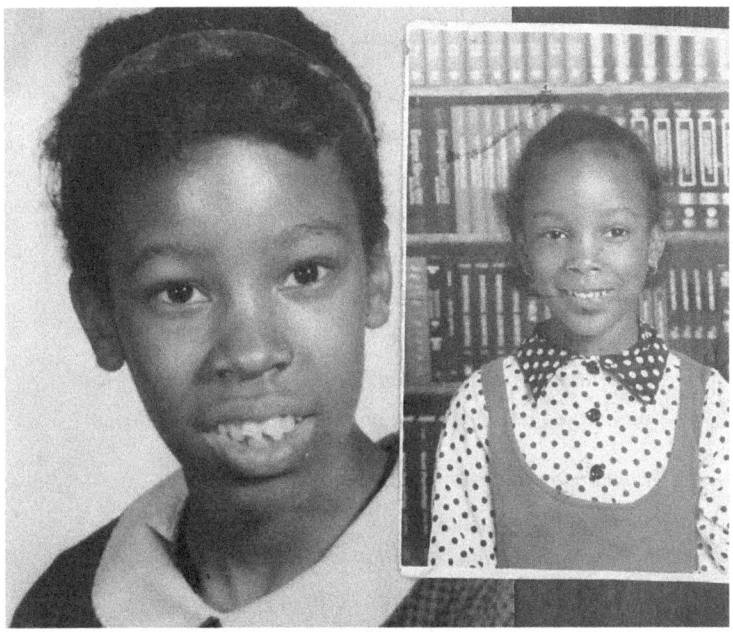

One thing that is very visible is my mom's two front teeth. They're chipped. She was playing in the classroom while in 1st grade and fell. Her parents didn't rush her to a dentist. Instead she was scolded for playing around in school and that was that.

My grandparents were poor and their main concerns for their kids were to provide food, shelter and clothing... the bare necessities. As long as those things were taken care of, then all was right with the world.

This was a major blow to her self-esteem...she was also super thin and was teased and bullied relentlessly. Those known and unknown scars stay with a child and my moms were both physical and emotional.

My moms teeth stayed like that until she went to the dentist for the first time in 1977 when she started working for IBM.

I remember the line in The Color Purple when Celie's father said to her as a child "Celie, you got the ugliest smile this side of Creation" and from that point forward she hid her smile often covering it with her hands anytime she laughed or smiled...until the scene in Shug's dressing room years later as an adult when Shug asked her..."Miss Celie, why you always covering up your smile?" In that moment, Celie was seen and began to come into her true self and realize her beauty on the inside and outside.

While my mom never stopped smiling, the impact of having to walk around with cracked teeth her entire childhood into her adult years took its toll in a number of ways. I'm not going to psychoanalyze but think about what becomes of a little black girl in this world who's flawed or broken in some way?

The following quote sums up to me where I think my mom is in her life right now or a big part of what makes her who she is today and what she has worked towards to become (I'll ask her after she reads today's post):

"I love people, I love the world, I love my nieces, I love my nephews, I love my family, I love them so deeply. But right now it's about me and little Mary. It's like that's my baby, my little girl. She needs my help...and I'm not going *to ever let anybody hurt her again." — Mary J Blige*

#celebratelifewithjoan #70DaysofJoan

"I know a girl named Joanie Maroni, she's as skinny as a stick of macaroni." That was one of the made up rhymes that I was constantly teased with starting in the first grade and it only got worse. One day I was playing around in the classroom and fell flat on my face, and broke my two front teeth. Our school nurse Mrs. Jeter wrapped up the broken pieces in tissue. We didn't know at the time that they were my permanent teeth.

JOAN IN THE 6TH GRADE, LOUIS L. REDDING SCHOOL.

There was no dropping everything to tend to my "emergency". I was alive, didn't have any broken bones and my basic needs were being met.

As long as those things were taken care of, then all was right with the world. Getting my teeth fixed wasn't a priority or an expense worthwhile. My teeth stayed that way...like jagged, broken pieces of Chiclets gum. It wasn't until 1977 when I was 25 years old and went to the dentist for the very first time that I was able to get them fixed.

Adding to that, Mom either made all of our clothes or we were given clothes from other people. Not a sign of being thrifty or environmentally conscious as it's thought of today, only a sign once again of how poor we were. On occasion, we were treated to a new dress from a store in Smyrna, DE called Silco Cut Price Department Store, which was a local discount store that sold everything from housewares to snacks to clothing and jewelry. The store no longer exists, but you couldn't tell me anything when I put on my new frock. Those times were far and in between.

This was a major blow to my already fragile self-esteem...I was super thin, shy, and withdrawn. I didn't want to be seen and couldn't look people in the eye. I didn't think I was pretty and my broken teeth were further proof of that. My mom also plaited my hair every day, but she never did it tight enough, so inevitably, I'd come home with loose hair and get in trouble for having my hair out. Those things only gave the mean girls more ammunition in their daily battle against me. Those known and unknown scars stay with a child and mine were now both physical and emotional. We didn't talk about mental health or why people acted the way they did. It never entered my mind to think that they saw a light in me that they only wanted to dim, I only saw and felt that they hated me and I didn't know what I had done to deserve such harsh treatment.

I never remembered my parents saying the actual words "I love you." Mom and Daddy were very strict and we were always getting beatings. We couldn't talk in church or point fingers for fear of getting beat. Many of our whoopings were from doing mischievous things...kids being kids, I suppose. One time Barbara and I sprayed water all over the clean sheets that mom had just put on the bed. Fun at the time, but we didn't think about the consequences. The worst part of it was having to get our own switch from the woods and when that wasn't an option, mom would use an ironing cord. She was a firm believer in the Old Testament scripture of the Bible where, in Proverbs 13:24, it says "He who spares the rod hates his son, but he who loves him is diligent to discipline him." Spare the rod, spoil the child was her mantra and we were disciplined for any minor transgression. Today it would be considered child abuse. I remembered sitting in Daddy's lap only once or twice as a child. He told me the story of the Titanic. In my mind, that was love, but I still craved more and would spend a good portion of my formative and adult years seeking the love I didn't feel that I was getting at home.

POST 29 OF 70

NO FEAR

We're at the height of swim season!

My mom didn't learn how to swim until she was in her 60s, but she made sure that Tanya and I learned to swim at an early age. We both took swim lessons before we were 6 and became strong confident swimmers in the pool (all depths) and ocean.

We spent our summer days in the pool and most of our summer camps involved swimming.

I don't recall ever asking my mom specifically why she never learned to swim when she was younger. I was keenly aware of the Jim Crow laws that were in place during her youth or it could have been a combination of factors...actually I'm going to ask her more today.

The point of my story is that it's never too late to learn something new and while she was afraid, she overcame her fear and achieved a goal she set for herself. She's not the best swimmer and has mentioned taking even more lessons.

Today I celebrate all the parents and kids who realize the importance of pool and swim safety and are taking the necessary steps to ensure their kids learn how to be confident swimmers and have fun along the way.

#celebratelifewithjoan #70DaysofJoan

Fear of dogs

One of my childhood traumas that still haunts me to this day is my fear of dogs. I mean I have an extreme fear and while it's gotten better over time, it's a slow process. When I was little, our neighbors had really mean dogs that they failed to keep tied up in their yard.

One day, I was walking up our lane and one of the dogs started chasing me. I fell down and it bit me on my thigh. I don't remember how I got away or who came to save me. Unfortunately it's a fear that I unknowingly passed along to my girls. I can't undo the past, but I can move forward to create a different outcome for tomorrow.

I think about my internalized fear of dogs when I reflect on some of the obstacles that I've had to deal with in life and what it took for me to get through or overcome them.

JOAN LEARNS TO SWIM AT AGE 60.

SOME HERO'S DON'T WEAR CAPES

There are two people in my mom's life who exemplify the true essence of the impact that teachers have on a child's life.

Ms. Bellamy and Ms. Winder were my mom's 1st grade teachers. They were just starting their teaching careers with Ms. Bellamy working initially as the class TA. They were 100+% committed to their responsibilities in educating and shaping young minds until their retirement.

To this day, my mom still keeps in touch with them...the teacher/student relationship transitioned into a special lasting friendship full of love, respect and admiration.

My mom picks each of them up for their monthly lunch outings. Ms. Bellamy is now 85 and Ms. Winder is now 97. They are just as sharp and ornery as ever from what I'm told and from my brief conversations with them. What's discussed during the outings stays at the table.

Tanya and I were blessed to have a similar relationship with one of our middle school teachers which still lasts to this day...Ms. B as we affectionately call her (Yvonne Boggus) has been a role model, friend and supporter since I was 13. She entrusted Tanya and I with the care of her 2 boys. She likes to tell the story that we were the only students she allowed to take care of her kids.

Today I'm celebrating the superheroes in our lives for their dedication, patience, and guidance in helping kids to imagine the best possibilities for their futures.

#celebratelifewithjoan #70DaysofJoan

BETTYE BELLAMY　　　　　　　　MARIAN WINDER

I've always believed that people are placed in your life for a reason and at a crucial time when I was shaping my views of my small world outside of my home life and drawing more into myself, there were two people who saw a light in me that I didn't yet know existed. Bettye Henry (now Bellamy) and Marian Harris Winder were my first grade teachers. They were just starting their teaching careers, with Miss Henry student teaching. Miss Henry was my savior and the first person I remember being kind to me. I cleaned the blackboards and erasers after class which was considered a high honor back in the day. I was always a good student and loved going to school. I especially loved reading. Miss Henry rode the same school bus with us each day and one day, she took me home with her, where she gave me my first book to read. I can't recall the book, but I remember that it was the first time I felt special. I was the only student that she ever took home with her. I ate dinner with her family and they all doted on me. Just the fact that she took her personal time with me made me feel that I mattered to someone outside of my family.

They were 100+% committed to their responsibilities in educating and shaping young minds until their retirement. To this day, we still keep in touch...the teacher/student relationship transitioned into a special lasting friendship full of love, respect, and admiration. We have a standing monthly lunch outing that's gone on now for close to ten years. At the time of this writing, Mrs. Bellamy is 87 and Mrs. Winder is 99. I still gain tons of wisdom from them. These are two people in my life who exemplify the true essence of the impact that teachers can have on a child's life.

JOAN WITH HER TEACHERS DURING ONE OF THEIR OUTINGS.

POST 31 OF 70

WE ARE FAMILY

Experiences not things...that's what kids truly remember about their parent(s). They can rarely recall the THINGS they received and I could list a number of things that could take up the entire space so you fill in your blanks.

Growing up, my family was far from rich in monetary terms but there was love and nurturing beyond measure. All of my needs were met and I was indulged from time to time growing up. I do like nice things but I've never been materialistic. I'm grateful to my mom for instilling the value of experiences over things...it's always been a part of my life.

When I reflect, I distinctly recall special moments both big and small...like waking up to the smell of my favorite breakfast, a day trip to the beach or park, waking up to dance music with my mom singing at the top of her lungs, my first trip to NYC (which is still my favorite city), my first concert at 11 (front row to see Patti LaBelle), first trip to Disney World at 6...I could go on and on.

So on this day, I'm celebrating the experiences and not the things. What will count in the end is not who's collected the most toys!

#celebratelifewithjoan #70DaysofJoan

I didn't realize that I had other sisters and brothers outside of my immediate four siblings until I was in my early teens. Mom married Daddy when she was 30, he was 50. She moved from New York City and wed into a ready-made family with step-children who were closer to her in age that they called her "Sis". One of my other siblings would often drop her kids off for mom to babysit and my nieces and nephews were more like close cousins and playmates. There was no talk of step mother or step siblings, we were all family. Fifteen of us all together. My niece Beverly was my best friend and playmate when we were little. My world expanded even more. Tommy, who was the eldest brother, would pick us up and take us to Sunday school. He would give us money and take us to Dairy Queen. For Christmas, he and his wife Beadie would bring us nuts, oranges, apples, and candy cane sticks. I thought he and my older brother William (Ham as we affectionately called him) were rich because they always drove nice cars and had money.

JOAN AND HER SIBLINGS AT FATHER'S 100TH BIRTHDAY CELEBRATION: SITTING:L-R: EUGENE MITCHELL, SARA SHOCKLEY, RALEIGH MITCHELL, JOAN MITCHELL STANDING L-R: DANIEL MITCHELL, GEORGE MITCHELL, ELIZABETH MITCHELL, WALTER MITCHELL, BARBARA MITCHELL-WILLIAMS, WILLIAM MITCHELL, DR. BEULAH MITCHELL, OSCAR MITCHELL.

We never believed in Santa Claus and didn't have regular toys like other kids, instead we'd play with stones and bricks outside. That all stopped when I got hit in my forehead with a brick and started bleeding. Thankfully it didn't leave a scar. Daddy would cut a tree from out back that we'd decorate with popcorn strings. I didn't get a toy until my sisters Beulah and Elizabeth started working when they were teenagers. My first toy was a white baby doll with three faces. When you turned her head, the face would change expressions. Creepy, I know, but I was excited and loved that doll.

My daily life as a young girl revolved around church, school, and work, and it was pretty much in that order. My parents were very religious and in the 6th grade I got saved, which means I gave my life to Christ. I couldn't truly comprehend that as a child. All I knew is that I didn't want to go to Hell. Going to Hell meant fire and brimstone and sounded like an awful place to end up if you sinned. I was fearful and felt it was something I had to do...we were never to question. I remember having to "tarry for the Holy Ghost" and repeating "Jesus, Jesus, Jesus" over and over again. Our family was heavily involved in the church. I sang in the choir and even though I couldn't sing, I was singing for the Lord. Growing up Pentecostal meant you couldn't wear makeup, jewelry, pants, or shorts. You had to wear long sleeves and have your head covered. We finally had a Victrola record player at home, but we could only listen to gospel music and not "the devil's music" as Mom used to call it. Again, I never questioned my parents, but spent years as an adult unlearning so many things I was taught as a child. I discovered that God is love and He is in all of us regardless of race, background, religion, or sexual orientation. I wondered how so many people could call themselves Christians while hating or speaking badly about others simply for who they were, what they looked like or who they loved, or where they came from. God made us all different, but God said He loved all mankind and that we should lead by example. I saw a lot of hypocrisy, but the one person I never saw it from was my mother. Essamond Turner Mitchell was the epitome of a Godly woman. When I was about six, I was asked what I wanted to be when I grew up and I would always say I wanted to be a missionary. When someone would tell me I didn't know what that meant, I would proudly say that it's someone who helps people. I saw my mother's life by example. She helped people even when our family was in need. We had a neighbor who would come to our house every Tuesday to get food and coffee.

I was still being teased and picked on in school, but there were several people who came to my rescue, showed me true kindness, and made my school days more bearable. There were several people outside of my family who saw the real me and made me feel comfortable. Victor and Vivian Perkins lived up the road from us and were always nice to me. In addition to my friend Helen Roy, Diana Clayton, Diana and Deborah "Debbie" Waters were my true, blue friends who I could trust and count on from day one. I remember that Diana would give me ten cents to attend the school dance on Fridays. I felt like she had given me a million dollars! Joyce Cale (Huggins) was also another friend and so nice to me. I stayed with her one weekend. They had so much food and milk, I thought they were rich. I've always valued my friendships and these early relationships, unbeknownst to me as a young girl, set the foundation for my friendships to this day. I have never met a stranger. Poet, activist, and memoirist Maya Angelou once said, "People will forget what you said, people will forget what you did, but people will never forget how you made them feel."

My day to day youthful life continued to evolve around home, church, school and work...pretty much in that order.

In addition to our constant chores around the house, which included cleaning the woodwork weekly, my family and I picked potatoes with migrant workers from Florida and local folk during the summer. We got paid a measly sum for grueling labor, but it was an honest day's work and I was happy for the money. During high school I babysat for Ida and Dallas Briscoe's kids and also cleaned. This gave me good practice as later on in my teen years, I helped Mom take care of my sister Liz's twins while she worked. On Saturday mornings I cleaned a white woman's house. Mrs. Grove would pick me up in the morning and I'd spend the day cleaning her house from top to bottom. I took pride in my work and she always complimented me on how well I cleaned. I never felt demeaned...it was part of my world. All I thought about was the money I made. I thought that Mrs. Grove was rich; she had so much jewelry. So much so that one day I took a black onyx ring from her jewelry box and gave it to my friend Norma Tribbitt as a gift. Mrs. Grove, to my knowledge, never noticed and I'm sure I would have been in big trouble if she did. I never thought of the consequences of someone finding out, but I lived with the guilt from the sin I committed for months.

My world began to expand even more when I entered junior high. Louis L.Redding Middle School. I sang in the choir, ran track, and loved to dance. I would beg my parents for permission to attend the dances with my niece Beverly. The school bus would pick us up and off we'd go. I was still very skinny and shy, but you couldn't tell me anything when I was on the dance floor. Still can't to this day! A pivotal moment for me occurred during our class trip to the New York World's Fair when I was in seventh grade. It was my first trip outside of Delaware without my family. This was way more exciting than the trips we took down to Capron, VA to visit with our aunt Hiddie during summer breaks. I was so excited to take in all the sites from the fair with my classmates, but in my wonderment, I became distracted and got separated from my group at the very beginning of the fair. Instead of enjoying the rides, I spent the entire time walking around trying to find my group. But the one thing I recall is that I wasn't afraid, only frustrated that I didn't get to truly experience the fair.

President John F. Kennedy was assassinated when I was in the sixth grade, I got my first black male teacher, Mr. Wright, and more importantly to my 13-year-old self was getting my first bra and also my period. When I told my mom that I started my period her exact words to me were "now you know you can't mess with the boys." That's all she said...no explanation and I didn't dare to ask her, so I just nodded and said ok. When I finally became interested in boys, I was in the eighth grade, but still had no understanding of how to interpret or process what I was feeling and I was also too afraid to ask.

Education was always stressed in our home. Both of my parents completed their schooling as young children. Mom made it all the way to the fourth grade and Daddy to the first grade, but both of them learned to read and write. They were proud and wanted their children to be educated. I was an honor roll student all the way through my schooling. People would pay me to help them with their homework or cheat on a test. I know, that's wrong, but that was also me helping people...my life's missionary work. I prided myself on perfect attendance and never missed a day of school. While my friends and older siblings were protesting and attending sit-ins, I was more concerned with getting my perfect attendance certificate. We never got involved in civil rights and when my parents voted, someone came around to tell them who to vote for and gave them a ride to cast their ballot followed by a monetary "donation" for their support. Mom and Dad never talked about race or racism.

I heard that my Daddy had to leave his home in Ahoskie, NC because he pulled a gun on a white man who didn't want to pay him, but my father was tight-lipped on most things from his past and never corroborated the story. I was curious about finding out the history of my father's side of the family after my cousin Eula Mae visited us and gave me a copy of an old article about my grandfather Jesse R. Mitchell. He was the last person lynched in Bertie County, North Carolina. The next year I drove my father and two oldest brothers Walter and Dan down to North Carolina for our annual trip to visit family. While we were there, I stopped at the local court house in Bertie County to inquire about my grandfather and the article I had read. Court records revealed that he was accused of killing his wife (my grandmother) and signed 60 acres of land over to his lawyer as collateral. He was swiftly found guilty and sentenced to death by lynching. Daddy was an orphan at the age of seven and was raised by his older sister Grover. When I came back to the car and asked Daddy why he never told us about what happened, his anger towards me was so intense. I had never seen him so mad. He told me I had no business digging up the past and that I needed to leave it alone, but for me it was a way to somewhat understand who my parents were as individuals. We knew very little about our mother's family...only that they hailed from Capron, Virginia and that she had one sister.

JOAN WITH HER PARENT'S AND SIBLINGS AT FATHER'S BIRTHDAY CELEBRATION
SITTING L-R: WALTER MITCHELL, LULA WILSON, RALEIGH MITCHELL, ESSAMOND MITCHELL, GEORGE MITCHELL, MARY LLOYD STANDING: RANDOLPH MITCHELL, ELIZABETH MITCHELL, EUGENE MITCHELL, DR. BEULAH MITCHELL, WILLIAM MITCHELL, JOAN MITCHELL, DANIEL MITCHELL, OSCAR MITCHELL, SARA SHOCKLEY, BARBARA MITCHELL-WILLIAMS.

OH BABY

This is where my story began.

As I mentioned in a previous post, my mom got pregnant with me when she was 16, gave birth to me when she was 17 and married my dad. She was an honor roll student, well-liked by her classmates, active in clubs and sports with plans of heading to college. Her parents (my mom mom and pop pop) were disappointed, but were 100% supportive even though they were staunchly religious. It was frowned upon to have a child out of wedlock during those times.

My mom left "regular" school and completed her senior year at James H. Groves and DAPI (Delaware Adolescent Program, Inc) which is an alternative fresh start for pregnant teens to receive the health & social services they need to continue education during and after pregnancy.

I was born prior to the Supreme Court of the United States's 1973 landmark decision in Roe v. Wade, and subsequent companion decisions, which made abortion legal but restricted by states to varying degrees.

And, while my mom was encouraged by some to get an abortion...something that she opposed for herself (as evidence of my being here), she is pro-choice...has always supported a woman's right to choose and firmly believes that a woman and her doctor, not politicians or the government should make the decision concerning a woman's body.

So today, in honor of my moms 70th birthday, I am making donations in her name to BOTH Planned Parenthood and DAPI.

Celebrating women who have made the difficult

decision to have an abortion AND also celebrating women who made the decision to bring a child into this world...the key word is DECISION. The reason "why" on both accounts is not my concern.

Honoring those who are fighting the good fight to protect abortion rights and accessible healthcare for all women.

#celebratelifewithjoan #70DaysofJoan

JOAN'S SENIOR PHOTO.

My life took an unexpected turn in 1969 which would prove to be the beginning of many pivotal moments. I met a young man who would later become my first husband, more so out of a sense of obligation and being the right thing to do when you knock someone up. Yes, me...pregnant at 16. Remember the non-sex talk that I had with my mother with her telling me that since I got my period, I can't mess with boys? Well my education (or lack thereof) didn't go that far from when I was 13.

Although I had friends, was active in various clubs and still managed to maintain my honor roll and high academic standards, I was still the shy little girl deep down inside seeking love and validation. I met Theodore during my sophomore year in high school. He was five years older than me and had already graduated from high school. My dating experience was pretty non-existent and here was an older guy who was nice to me and showed me attention. I instantly fell for him. Theodore was already working, had money in his pockets, and he was creative. I told him the story of my mother giving me my first camera when I was in junior high. I loved that camera, but it got destroyed. Theodore brought me a new camera. It was the first gift I ever received from a man. My parents were still very strict, but they allowed me to go out. I had to be home by 10 pm, but there's a lot kids can do before curfew and I was a classic example. Theodore and I didn't date long, but he took me to my junior prom when I was in the 11th grade. I remember I had on a green gown with yellow flowers. I felt like a princess. We left early from the prom and went to his sister's house. I had sex for the first time...I was a virgin and got pregnant that night. When I didn't get my period, Theodore gave me money to see a doctor who confirmed that I was indeed pregnant. I only told my niece Beverly, but her mother, my sister-in-law Rachel, figured it out and told my mom. My parents were hurt and upset, but dealt with the hand they were given.

TANYA AND TERESKA.

When I told Theodore I was pregnant, he immediately said that we had to get married to give the child a name. While a few of his family members urged me to abort the baby, my mom rallied to the occasion and told me that I didn't have to get married and that she and my father would help me to raise my child. I was already embarrassed and disappointed in myself, but I never thought once about not going through with the pregnancy. Theodore gave me a small ring, I transferred to a school for pregnant girls and on November 1, 1969, wearing a pink dress and green coat, I became Mrs. Theodore Thomas. I went to DAPI (Delaware Adolescent Program, Inc.) during the day and attended James H. Grove at night to finish my high school education where I received a GED. I still had hopes of attending college, but with a few fits and starts as a new wife and mother, that dream would elude me for another 30 years when I finally graduated with a B.A. in Human Resources Management from Wilmington University in 2005 at 42 years old.

My first daughter, Tereska was born just five months after we got married and we settled into our life as a new family. We lived with Theodore's sister for a month and then my sister Liz helped us to get an apartment at Monroe Park Apartments in Greenville, DE. They didn't let black people stay there at the time, but Liz called in a favor from one of her clients. Theodore wanted five kids and I immediately got pregnant with my second daughter, Tanya. Tanya was born just shy of a year from Tereska...literally 361 days apart. As soon as I had Tanya, I went on birth control pills and didn't tell my husband. I hid them in the closet bathroom.

The signs were always there, but I didn't heed the warning. Before we were married, Theodore and I attended a friend's wedding. He flew into a jealous rage because I was simply talking to another man. He screamed and berated me for being disrespectful and flirting. While it was far from the truth, he was blinded by jealousy. I knew that there was something majorly wrong, but I felt trapped into following through with the marriage because I was pregnant. He later apologized which would become a pattern and excuse for his behavior. The first time Theodore hit me was after we were married. I shouldn't have been surprised as the verbal and emotional abuse were evident early on in our relationship. Stunned and afraid for my life, I called the police. Instead of arresting him, he opted for them to place him under a 72 hour hold at the state hospital. It was his way of getting out of trouble and not being charged with domestic violence. What was more troubling is the state trooper telling me that he could see why my husband was so jealous...it was because I was so pretty.

My mother said that if a man hits you, he doesn't love you. I lived in constant fear and walked on eggshells. Anything could set him off and I had no way of knowing exactly when and where he'd be triggered. I had two little girls under the age of three and I was in survival mode. I made sure to present the picture of a happy family and loving couple on the outside, but at home, my life was a living hell.

The last time he hit me was the worst; not because of the beating, but because he did it in front of my girls. Tereska and Tanya were eating breakfast at the kitchen table. It all happened so fast. I attended an anniversary celebration for a co-worker one evening. No spouses were in attendance, only employees. There was a picture of me sitting next to a male co-worker. I hid the pictures from the party, but Theodore found them and accused me of cheating on him. He flew into a rage and started punching and kicking me. I yelled for the girls to go to their mom-mom and pop-pop's house. We lived in a trailer behind my parents. The girls ran across the field to safety. My dad was ready to get his gun and kill Theodore.

Enough was enough and I knew it was finally time to leave. My girls needed me and I didn't want them to see me living this way. This was not love, it was abuse. I was afraid to live in the trailer alone, so Mom would stay with us every night after Theodore moved out so that I would feel safe and try to sleep.

JOAN AND HER GIRLS.

I lived in constant fear for a long time that he would kill me and make good on his words that if he couldn't have me, then no one could. Not too long after we divorced, I read a news story about a woman who was killed by her boyfriend while she was at work. What sent chills down my spine from reading the article was that the victim worked for one of my former employers, Du Pont Haskell Lab. What made it even more eerie was that she had my previous job and also sat at the same desk. All I kept thinking was that could have been me. My fear didn't subside until Thedore remarried. I never discussed what happened with my girls, but as an adult, my daughter Tereska vividly recounted that fateful day where she witnessed Theodore beating me in the living room while she and Tanya sat at the kitchen table. She was only three.

Theodore's family was very angry with me. They didn't believe in divorce and immediately turned on me...telling me that my girls were going to grow up to be nothing without a father in the home. Those hurtful words and sentiments made me determined to prove them wrong. I didn't harbor any hate in my heart and made sure the girls spent time with their father and had a relationship with him. Even though he disregarded the court order to pay a measly fifty dollars a month in child support after our divorce was final, I never took him back to court. After he remarried, he had two more children with his new wife adding to her existing two children from her previous marriage. Through the years, we were cordial with each other...never friendly, but got along for the sake of our girls. Prior to his death in 2003 he apologized and thanked me for doing a great job. I had long forgiven him, more so for my peace of mind and happiness.

POST 50 OF 70

THE MEN

My mom's been married 5 times and while I was hesitant at first to give her permission to go for a 6th, I now say to her "do it as many times as YOU want." Granted I'm not trying to have her be a nurse or a purse, so putting that out there right now.

She used to be ashamed to divulge the number of marriages and was concerned about other people's opinions, but listen here...that's the beauty in this life... getting to the age or stage where you're able to live your truth and be 100% unapologetic. Mother has lived.

It took my mom close to 70 years to get to this point and her wish for me is to not take that long to live my authentic life and not concern myself with the "people".

Shout out to hubby #3 Tyrone Brown. While they've been divorced for YEARS, they remain the dearest of friends, hang out and IMO bicker like an old married couple. We love Tyrone and he's still family and will always be as far as we're concerned!

I've gone off track because this post was supposed to be about my mom celebrating the symbolism of marriage in a unique way. She married herself on 12/13/14 in a beautiful water-side soul ceremony which I performed (also wrote the vows) and De'Andre and Grayson witnessed. The boys were confused, but they went along with the program. They helped collect items from nature for the bouquet as we walked to our destination.

I used to keep a quote by Susan L. Taylor (former Editor-in-Chief of Essence Magazine) where she said "Give yourself to yourself before you give yourself away." That

> *quote can be interpreted many ways, but for me, it's my mom's commitment to love herself, honor herself and be the best person for herself whether she's with a partner (or not) and that is why I celebrate her today.*

One of my sisters recently asked me, "When did you get so selective with choosing men?" after I asked her questions about a man that she was trying to set me up with, but knew absolutely nothing about. He was a man, breathing and available...I should be okay with that, right? I was taken aback and her words actually stung. But when I reflected on why her statement bothered me so much, it was because in hindsight, I asked myself, did she have a point?

According to a Washington Post article from 2015 titled Millions of Americans have been married three times or more, "serial marriage is a lot more common than you might think in the U.S. According to Census data from 2013, over 9 million Americans have been married three times or more. That works out to roughly 5.3 percent of the total married population. Or, put it this way: more than 1 in every 20 married Americans has taken three or more trips to the altar."

While I never gave it much thought, I'm in a league with some of my all time favorite Hollywood legends...who married multiple times. Zsa Zsa Gabor (married nine times), Elizabeth Taylor and Lana Turner (married eight times each), Rue McClanahan (married seven times), and Liza Minelli and Diahann Carroll (married four times each) have all shared their thoughts on love and marriage. But the words that impacted me the most came from my all-time favorite award-winning actress, singer, model, and activist, Diahann Carroll. In one of Oprah's Master Class on OWN, Diahann Carroll talked about her marriages. I'm paraphrasing, but she spoke about learning to live alone, learning about herself and looking inward to answer questions about herself. She called out that the choices you make for your life are yours alone. One of the most profound things she pointed out was how she expected these men to make her extremely happy when she couldn't make herself extremely happy. She said she was an old lady before she learned that lesson. At 70, I wouldn't call myself an old lady, but Diahann and I are on the same page when it comes to learning how to make yourself happy and not being dependent on someone else.

Each of the men I married and the relationships I've had throughout my life have taught me lessons about myself and some hard truths that at times I didn't want to face. I've experienced tremendous joy and heart-wrenching pain, but through it all, I had no regrets and still believed in love.

JOAN AND HER SECOND HUSBAND, JOHN.

Confession: there's another reason why I have an affinity and connection to Diahann Carroll. I met my soon-to-be second husband in 1976 at a disco club in Newark, DE. I was on a date with a guy at the Hotel du Pont in the Brandywine Room. After the date, I left to go dancing with friends. While I was at the club a guy approached me and said I looked like Diahann Carroll. I was flattered of course, but ironically, that same night, I met John Harvey who also used the same pick up line and said I looked like Diahann Carroll. Hey, I'll take it! John was very easy on the eyes. He had golden brown skin, soft brown wavy hair and a slight gap between his beautiful white teeth. His slight southern accent was still evidence of his Alabama roots. John and I danced the night away and we had a great time. He was an amazing dancer, which I loved immediately. At the end of the evening, he asked me for my number. I wouldn't give him my number, but told him to give me his and said I would call him.

It took me two weeks to finally call John. When I called, I said "hello this is Diahann." I said it as a joke in reference to his pick-up line, but he said you don't sound like Diane...mixing me up with another woman. We had a good laugh and made plans to go out the next night to Dover Air Force Base. From there we started dating and became exclusive rather quickly. John and I clicked immediately. He loved to cook and entertain, and was so much fun. My daughters took to John right away. I was hesitant to bring another man around them given my experience with their father, but from day one, he treated them with loving care as if they were his own and they loved him. We moved into Iron Hill Apartments in Newark, DE together and settled into our new reality. John's daughter Wanda from his first marriage would stay with us during the weekends. My girls were in first and second grade and Wanda was going into middle school. John wanted to get married, but I flat out told him no. I never wanted to get married again and painfully told him what

I went through in my first marriage. He despised Theodore for what he did to me and the fact that it left me so damaged. I was dead set against marriage and made it hard for John to break through my barrier. Famous last words.

At the time, I was working for Getty Oil Credit Card in Newark, DE at University Park. They announced that they were closing the office, but offered everyone jobs, including working at the oil refinery in Delaware City. I decided to take the job since the pay was good. No women had ever worked outside as a refinery operator. The hours were long and I eventually became the first one to leave the job because of scheduling conflicts. I couldn't be home in the morning to get the girls up for school and it became too stressful as John, who worked at Chrysler Auto, also had a demanding schedule and worked long hours. Even though I enjoyed the job, took pride in my work and loved the money, my girls came first.

John and I were happy and the last thing I had on my mind was meeting another man, let alone at work. I met Brooks Stevens who also worked as a refinery operator. He was married with kids. That should have stopped me from the go, but we were drawn to each other in a way that I had never felt for another man, not even John. Brooks was fun and exciting. He was big and strong...people always mistook him for "Mean" Joe Greene, who played football for the Pittsburgh Steelers. He was worldly with a warm, down home feel. Brooks made me feel special and exposed me to experiences that I had only dreamed of at the time. We became hot and heavy very quickly and would spend as much time together as possible, sneaking around town—which you can only do but so much in small town Delaware. We'd meet and spend hours together talking, making love...whatever we wanted to do with our stolen moments. To me, it wasn't a fling, we were in love. I eventually introduced him to my girls and just like with John they took to him, but never said a word or questioned about our lives with John and what all of this adult stuff meant. They had two men in their lives who treated them like princesses and cared for them, and not just to get in good with me. The girls loved riding around in his sports car and listening to his vast music collection. Brooks had an album collection to rival most DJs with all types of music, from R&B, jazz, rock, to country & western.

John suspected that I was cheating and I took dangerous chances to be with Brooks. A friend of John's lived next to Brooks and told him that I was cheating on him. One day, John tracked me and Brooks down at my sisters apartment and began banging on the door. Brooks and I were in the shower when we heard the banging. I didn't answer, but John knew I was there with someone. He eventually left and went home. We broke up and went our separate ways. Brooks wanted to leave his wife and kids so that we could be together, but I told him no. I couldn't let him ruin his family. They didn't deserve it and I would have felt even more awful for breaking up a family.

A few months after John and I broke up, he reached out to me and told me how much he really loved and cared for me. John and I started dating each other again and I broke things off with Brooks. Although we remained good friends until he passed away in 2021, Brooks and I only remained friends and were never romantically involved. He respected my marriages and valued our friendship more than anything. He still kept up with the girls and they often spoke of their fond memories. Not until they were much older, did they fully realize the dynamics of what happened during their youth. We had a lot of laughs and lectures of don't do what I did, but also, live your life. I also got to know Brooks' wife and kids throughout the years. I have no idea what Brooks said to his wife about me, but I also don't know any other women, black or white, who would have tolerated another woman in her husband's life. It seemed that there was an unspoken knowing that we all lived with and existed in for many years. I went to see Brooks in the hospital on his deathbed. His wife called to let me know his time was near. When I got to the hospital, the first thing he said was "what took you so long?" He'll always be cherished as one of my greatest loves, but John was my soulmate.

John and I were happy, but still not married, much to his chagrin. I was working for IBM as an executive assistant in their Wilmington, DE office. I was offered a promotion, but had to relocate to Valley Forge, PA. It was our first time living outside of Delaware and the girls once again went along with the plan and made the adjustment.

John and Wanda would drive up on the weekends, but it was difficult to maintain a long distance relationship with the demands of work and kids. We decided that they'd move to Valley Forge and live with us. Wanda was living with John full time and in high school. We enrolled her at Great Valley High School and Tereska and Tanya attended K.D. Markley Elementary School in Malvern. We weren't in Pennsylvania for long as two things occurred. The first was that our rental office found out that John and Wanda weren't on the lease after I reported an incident about a few of the neighborhood kids bullying my girls. Secondly, John found out that he was sick and was diagnosed with leukemia. We decided to move back to Delaware and I continued working for IBM in the Wilmington office. John's cancer was aggressive and in April of 1981, John's doctor told him to get his affairs in order. Once again he asked me to marry him and this time I said yes. By that time, we had been together for a little over six years. One of the most excruciating experiences is to watch someone you love slowly deteriorate day after day. The cancer ravaged John's body and showed no mercy on a man who was once a vibrant and healthy young man.

John was just 37 when he passed. At one point we thought we had all the time in the world...our lives were just getting started. Before John passed, he asked me to raise Wanda even though her mother was still alive. I promised him that I would. Shortly after John passed, Wanda's mother came with the police to get Wanda, but Wanda told them that she wanted to stay with me. I treated Wanda as if she were my own. There was no step-daughter. She was my eldest daughter, Tereska, the middle (not the oldest anymore) and Tanya, my baby. My relationship with Wanda's mother was acrimonious and there was a bitter hatred conveyed towards me that to this day, still baffles me. I began dating John long after they were divorced. I kept my promise to John. Wanda has two mothers and I've continued to respect the relationship that she's built with her birth mother through her adult life, even when it's meant me swallowing my pride and not expressing my disappointment when I haven't been acknowledged alongside Wanda's birth mother during some of Wanda's pivotal life moments.

Before John got sick, he never went to church and although I was raised in the church and saved as a youth, going to church was only something I did on occasion as an adult in my twenties and early thirties. When John got sick, he started going to church and "got right with the Lord" as the old folks say. He didn't want to die and believed that God could heal him. We all wanted a miracle. I needed something to ground me in this moment and the Mother Church of God in Christ was the balm I needed.

I was still a young mom carrying the weight of the world on my shoulders and now a widow at 36. My life now revolved around work, church, and my three girls. I became a devout Christian. My grief and newfound religion opened up a vulnerability in me that I was too naïve to recognize, and created the ideal scenario or perfect storm for my next relationship. Samuel O'Brien was a minister at our church who visited and prayed with John while he was sick. Not too long after John passed, Samuel latched onto me and offered comfort. I embraced his attention and fell quickly into the dutiful girlfriend role. My girls could not stand Samuel and expressed how they felt time and time again, but I wouldn't listen. They wanted to see me happy, so they tolerated our relationship. Samuel quickly weaseled his way into our family and I made it easy for him. I cooked huge Sunday dinners after church and always served him first. He got the biggest piece of fried chicken. I also loaned him large sums of money and let him drive my car. Today they'd call that stuck on stupid, but I truly believed that our relationship was blessed by God and that He sent Samuel to me. Samuel asked me to marry him at my sister Liz's wedding reception in Atlanta, GA with a ring that I later found out was purchased by his mother. I accepted his proposal and my girls cried, but they were not happy tears. The long drive from Georgia back to Delaware was a solemn one and also smelly as Samuel had the most awful gas which could kill a skunk. It didn't matter to me...I was going to marry a minister and become the perfect Christian wife.

JOAN AND HER GIRLS; TERESKA, WANDA AND TANYA.

Ironically, maybe my girl's collective prayers were answered. Not too long after we got engaged, I heard rumors that Samuel was seeing someone else. Apparently she knew about me, but not vice-versa. It just so happened that she worked at a store where I was shopping one day. Unbeknownst to me, I went to her checkout line and she saw my name on the credit card. It was a scene straight out of Jill Scott's song "Exclusively" where she waxed poetically...

> "At the market the people were pushing and shoving
> Trying to be the next in line, the turn was mine
> The new girl at the counter was cute, but not as fine as me
> Was this some kind of woman's intuition, some kind of insecurity
> Nah, 'cause my man is happy at home loving me exclusively
> So I shook my head, "whats up?"
> "Hello, "she smiled as she rung me up
> Orange juice $3.29, Croissants $4.85
> She sniffed, Butter 89 cents
> She sniffed, Strawberries $1.50 a pint
> She sniffed, and sniffed, and sniffed, and sniffed again
> And then replied, "Raheem, right?"
> "Right."

In this case, it was Samuel O'Brien. Whew...I dodged a bullet and my girls were ecstatic, but I never got my money back. We never communicated after that incident and that was the final straw.

My longest relationship with a man was with someone I've known for over 50 years. He was actually my first crush. I met Tyrone Brown at Middletown High School. We passed each other in the hall one day and he asked me for a piece of doublemint chewing gum. We were both shy, but really liked each other. He was able to get his father's car to take me out for our one and only date in high school. We went to dinner and afterwards, he tried to get fresh with me and I refused his advances. He ended up taking me home early and we never connected again because he was sent to Vietnam not long after our connection.

JOAN AND TYRONE'S WEDDING, (L-R, TYRONE'S DAUGHTER TYLISA, JOAN'S DAUGHTERS, TERESKA, WANDA AND TANYA).

When Tyrone returned from Vietnam, I was married with my first child. He came to see me one day when Theodore wasn't home. My niece Beverly was with us. We chatted like old friends and continued as friends for years, although we didn't speak or see each other often. As fate would have it, almost twelve years after our first date and reconnection after his tour in Vietnam, Tyrone started attending the church we belonged to...the Mother Church of God in Christ, which we were still members of after John passed. He was seeing someone who went there, but they weren't serious. He was divorced and living at his mother's house in Townsend, DE. I decided to call him because I knew him to be trustworthy and very religious. We began talking, but our connection was once again interrupted as Samuel O'Brien was in hot pursuit and drew my attention away. Once Samuel and I broke up, Tyrone and I began dating in 1983 and married in 1985 after a very short engagement. We were legally married for ten years and during that time, I often questioned my marriage and lamented over whether Tyrone and I should have just remained friends.

I often think back to the times when he looked out for Mom, his mother-in-law. He treated her like she was his own mother. Mom lived with us on and off throughout our marriage. When mom had a massive stroke and was placed in a nursing home, he would visit with her constantly and read the Bible to her.

Tyrone was one of my dearest friends and until his passing, we bickered like an old married couple. I can honestly say that Tyrone was genuine through and through. I won't go into the intimate details of our marriage to protect his privacy and the memories of our friendship. I will say that we both had very different communication styles, which was at the root of many of our issues. Interestingly enough, the pastor who married us predicted that communication would be a problem with us.

My fourth and fifth husbands were basically the same man (well, not exactly). It was only when my fifth husband Jerald passed did I finally sit down and take stock of my role and how I contributed to creating this false sense of security and happiness. I was always good with making things look good on the outside, while suffering silently in pain and unhappiness on the inside. I learned to do that in my first marriage. I hadn't healed, but unknowingly internalized the trauma I had gone through with Theodore.

With husbands four and five, I felt self-conscious about my weight and my two front teeth, once broken off in grade school and now gapped and protruding after being "fixed." But, these men picked me, they told me I was beautiful and I was so happy to be chosen and loved. I made them look good...I made them the prize and played my role to a tee. It took me a long time to realize and know for myself without someone having to tell me that I am the prize and that I am beautiful.

I wasn't being fulfilled in my marriage to Tyrone and felt that I had done everything possible to save the marriage. One night we went to Atlantic City with my girlfriend Vivian and her boyfriend Cruz (they were dating, but weren't married yet). I remember trying to hold hands with Tyrone and he flat out refused. I'm affectionate and enjoy PDA, so this felt like a rejection. Not only were we not communicating, but we also had different love languages and neither one of us knew how to bridge the gap to where we needed to be to sustain and fix what was already broken. I confided in Vivian and told her about what was going on in my marriage. I hadn't shared with anyone else and even my girls were in the dark.

My girlfriend invited me to attend a trip to visit Martha's Vineyard with her church. During the trip, Vivian introduced me to a member of their church. His name was Philip Elliott. The first thing he said to me was "what's a beautiful young woman like you doing here all by yourself?" I was flattered by the attention. We planned to go dancing that evening, but my friends backed out. Philip said he'd go with me, but changed his mind as we'd already had a long day. He said he wanted to keep in touch after the trip and we began talking. He was a divorced, retired Philadelphia Stock Exchange unioned blue collar worker who had four children and three grandchildren. He was taking care of his mother who lived with him. A few weeks later, I went to visit Vivian's church in Philadelphia and Philip was sitting next to her. I later found out that Vivian told Philip everything that I shared with her about Tyrone. I was ripe for the picking and ready. After we ate Sunday dinner, Philip asked me to go for a walk in the park. We talked and strolled along enjoying the day. At one point, he pulled me into his arms and kissed me. He asked me if I had to go back home because he wanted to make love to me. I followed him to a hotel on City Line Avenue but ended up not going in. I was feeling guilty, yet excited and couldn't stop thinking about him. When I got home, I called him from the kitchen and made plans to see him again the following week. That Sunday, I drove to Philly to attend church and afterwards, he invited me over to his house. We made passionate love and Philip was so affectionate. I was smitten.

I would go to New York with him to visit his mom and aunt and he doted on me by buying me gifts. He always had a drink ready for me when I arrived. One time I surprised him by driving up to Philadelphia in nothing but a raincoat. We didn't make it to the bedroom, but ended up making love on the bathroom floor of his apartment. Our affair went on for a while and I finally told Tyrone that I wasn't happy and couldn't be with him anymore. He didn't express any emotion, but I knew that I hurt him. I hadn't been happy for a long time and was ready to move on with my life.

I told the girls about Philip and introduced them to him before I decided to leave Tyrone. They weren't too keen on him, but respected my decision. Plus, his being much older than me was another concern for them, but I was in love. Philip and I secretly got married and told my girls over a surprise dinner that evening at Shaffer's

Canal House. I figured breaking the news at one of their favorite restaurants would lessen the blow. It didn't, but once again, they only wanted me to be happy and called him Mr. Elliott out of respect for him. By this time, the girls were well into their teen years and had their own lives and interests.

After we got married, Philip moved to our house in Townsend, DE. His mother passed after a long battle with diabetes before we got married. Once he moved in, Philip immediately pressured me to put his name on the house. When I refused, Philip showed a side of himself that I had not witnessed before...meanness. Not hurt, upset or disappointed, but cruel.

He eased into life in Delaware and began attending church at Bethel Smyrna with my brother William "Ham." Ham loved him and everyone in the church did too. Image was very important. He wanted to impress people and put on his best for people to see. I took him to Boyd's in Philadelphia which is a famously known luxury retail store. I purchased a new suit and sports jacket for him on my credit card. I hadn't even spent $1,000 dollars on myself for clothes. He was getting a social security check each month, but blew through his money as he played the lottery all the time.

Philip also needed a new car, but when they ran his credit, it wouldn't go through. When they ran mine, bingo. The loan was in my name, but the title was in his and he paid the monthly car payment. He got a white Lincoln Town Car with a green top. Around the same time, my car was going bad and I made the decision to turn it in as a voluntary repossession. Philip wouldn't let me drive his car, so I ended up buying an old station wagon from a family friend. I needed something reliable. Here Philip was riding around showing off in a new car and I was driving a beat up station wagon. Philip wasn't well off financially and I discovered that he wasn't taking care of his mom before she passed, but it was quite the opposite. She was taking care of him and now I was doing the same. Can you say bamboozled?

Once again I ignored my intuition. I saw the signs before we were married, but chose to ignore them. Remember, he picked me. I mistook his jealously as flattery. He was afraid that I was still in love with Tyrone although I assured him that wasn't the case. I was also in school part-time finishing up my college degree. Philip was against me getting my diploma and was in the hospital due to complications from his Type 2 diabetes the night of my graduation. He was also upset that I didn't change my last name to his and would always say that he wished I loved him like I loved my girls. One time I went to California to visit my girlfriend Jean Garner for a week and he got mad at me for leaving him with no heat. The house didn't have a heating system at the time, but there were space and kerosene heaters.

JOAN GRADUATING COLLEGE AT 53.

I hated guns, still do, and Philip kept a 45 magnum pistol. Philip was a recovering alcoholic who still drank on occasion and he was a mean drunk. His son told me that his father had always been a mean S.O.B. and verbally abusive during the entire time he was married to his ex-wife. At the time, I didn't believe it, but very quickly realized that I was in the same predicament. History repeating itself in more ways than one.

The beginning of the end started not too long after we married. Philip accused me of running other men, in particular a long-time family friend who he also knew and considered a friend. I went to get some vegetables one day from our friend's garden and when I came home, he was enraged. To intimidate me, he asked me where his gun was, but I had taken it and hidden it downstairs in the basement where he couldn't find it.

By this time, I started sharing with my daughter Tereska what was going on and she encouraged me to leave, but I wasn't ready. I was ashamed and embarrassed. I was on husband number four and was consumed by what people would think.

I even distanced myself from one of my closest friends and mentors, Ms. Bettye Bellamy, because she had given me a pamphlet on domestic violence. Was there a chink in my armor? Had she seen something I didn't want anyone to see?

The universe set things in motion when Philip went to his hometown in South Carolina to visit a woman who he hadn't seen in over 40 years. They used to date and she had his child, but he never saw or supported her, even though he knew he had a daughter. This was new to me, but at this point, nothing surprised me.

Philip and I were no longer sleeping in the same room and hadn't been intimate in years. Our days and nights filled with passion abruptly ended as soon as we got married. Literally from day one. He knew exactly what to do to get me and I fell head first right into his trap.

The final straw came one night when I went out with friends to go dancing and see my favorite band. I got in at one o'clock in the morning and Philip was still up with his door open. He was drinking and yelled out "you're nothing but a whore, you're no damn good." I said "you're no longer my husband and I'm no longer your wife." I went into my bedroom and locked my door. He tried to apologize, but I was done and the marriage was over.

He became even more mean and mentally abusive, but I still decided to stay married. Many women do it and I understand why. I don't judge someone for the decisions one makes about their marriage. No one but God knows what goes on behind closed doors. He lived his life and I lived mine. We didn't talk. We were roommates and I resigned to live my life that way. My daughter Tereska begged me to get a divorce because she was concerned that I didn't have peace in my own home and as long as he was in my space. Keeping the peace is not the same as real peace.

In my own time, I finally decided to divorce him in 2007 after we had been legally married for ten years. I was working for Bank of America/Fleet Bank at the time and used my pre-paid legal benefit. My attorney told me that because I had a good job and made more money, Philip could get alimony because that was the law. Philip was smug and said "you're not going to get out of this as easy as you think." I looked him dead in the eye and told him that if he tried to get a dime from me that he'd be sorry. I filed the papers, but when the court tried to serve him the papers, he was conveniently never home. After I told them what time he'd definitely be home, they were able to serve him. He didn't protest and our divorce became final on June 29, 2007. I gave him one month to get out of the house.

Hallelujah, I was free!

Philip was still in contact with his old flame and had started talking to his daughter. He was planning his next move and I was happy to be rid of him. He and his daughter decided that he would move to Georgia to live with her. She was excited to finally have a relationship with her father. I booked him a one way ticket departing on August 1st to Georgia and never saw him again. He left his car, TV and most of his clothes. After he was there for a month, his daughter called me and said "I don't know how you lived with him." He was so mean and evil. I didn't talk to her that much and never spoke to him. On October 31st, Philip died of a massive heart attack in his daughter's car as she was taking him to the doctor.

When he passed away, I had to get involved since I was still listed as his beneficiary. His four children wanted him back in Philadelphia, so I signed everything over to his daughter and told her to keep the remaining money after the expenses to fly his body back to Philly. His daughter came down from Philly to get his clothes and his daughter from Georgia came to get his car. I signed the car over to her, but never met her in person. I just left the car and everything in my yard for her to pick up.

While I was still legally married to Philip, I started seeing another older gentleman. I met Jerald Baker while I was out on a night of dancing to my favorite band. He was a widower whose wife had passed two years prior. Jerald had a first grade education but was self-taught, very intelligent, and a stickler for proper grammar. Even with the use of prosthetics from both of his legs being amputated due to a circulatory disease, he stood over 6 feet tall and commanded attention. Jerald had a huge presence and people were drawn to his smile and warm, bubbly personality. I was one of those people and was once again immediately smitten. He met my daughters. Tereska was living in New York City by this time and came to Delaware for a surprise birthday party that his daughter was having for him. Jerald looked dapper in his tuxedo and I was happy to be his girlfriend.

I didn't have any intention of getting married again, but Jerald proposed to me not too long after my divorce became final. The night he proposed, he said, "I've never seen you look so beautiful tonight. I want to spend the rest of my life with you. You'd make me the happiest man on earth." He told me that he didn't talk to my daughters, but said that they knew how he felt about me. I said yes, but he had one stipulation: it had to be on his birthday, which was also my daughter Tanya's birthday, February 7th.

We had a small wedding, and I was so excited because this was my first real one. Although I was married four times prior, I had never worn a traditional wedding dress. I wanted the day to be perfect; complete with the right dress and hair. I was overjoyed and Jerald was happy. We planned to go on a cruise for our honeymoon and I purchased a beautiful nightgown. Our first night as husband and wife was supposed to be a magical night to remember, but it was a memory that set the tone for our marriage. And at that moment, I knew I made a monumental mistake by marrying Jerald. We had intercourse prior to our marriage, so there was no question in my mind that on our wedding night of all nights, we'd make love. I put on my new nightgown and tried to get close to him. He flat out told me no and said that he was too weak and couldn't do "that". We didn't have sex for our entire marriage. Instead he bought me two dildos to satisfy my needs and his go-to choice for pleasure was masturbating to porn videos. We were lovey dovey in public...always affectionate with each other. He used to say that people probably think we're having sex all of the time. Outward appearances were important to him and I put on a front that everything was perfect.

We'd do date night every Thursday night in Rehoboth beach at 1776 and attended their New Year's Eve celebration for two years in a row. The staff and patrons loved Jerald. It was good for his ego and he reveled in the attention.

I was the dutiful, submissive wife and wanted this marriage to last. I would do anything I needed to do in order to be happy. I became Jerald's caregiver and he demanded that my primary focus was on him. When we met, I was working in Wilmington at the Hotel du Pont. I loved my job and co-workers. It was an ideal combination of everything that I enjoyed doing. I worked in the sales department as an administrative assistant. I interacted with our corporate clients on a daily basis and also worked with our hospitality group for event planning. After we got married, Jerald and I moved to Dover, DE, and lived with his daughter, son-in-law, granddaughter, and her two children for a year. He didn't force me, I volunteered and wanted him to be near his family. Plus, I was in awe of the neighborhood's man-made pond, of which we had a direct view from the backyard.

My daughter Tanya, who was 35 at the time, and her family had recently sold their house and were living at our family home in Townsend. With Jerald surrounded by his family every day, I felt better going to work and being away from home. Jerald wasn't thrilled about my schedule and wanted me to be closer to home. I decided to leave the Hotel du Pont and said that the commute was too much. I had just gotten a raise and promotion. They begged me to stay and couldn't understand why I'd leave. I ended up taking a job with the State of Delaware in Dover, DE and hated every minute. It was the most toxic environment that I've ever worked in...even worse than the job where I went in one weekend and left a note on my manager's desk that I quit. The people were certifiably crazy in my opinion, and I wore a mask everyday to hide how I really felt. I was an expert...I did it at home, so why not at work?

Like Philip, Jerald also had a mean streak and I never knew what would trigger his negative behavior towards me. Did I talk too much, not make his meal the way he liked it, or fail to iron his shirt the way he wanted? Anything could set him off and I tolerated it. I always wanted to keep the peace. When we were out, he'd flirt with the ladies and be sweet as pie.

Living in a house with three other adults wasn't easy and probably not one of the brightest ideas. At times, I felt that there were three people in the marriage. Jerald's daughter Sabrina and I were close in age and she was extremely close to her dad. They told each other everything and talked all the time. Sabrina and I got along, but she was always daddy's girl and let me know that she was number one. I was just the wife. I went along to get along and made it a point to go above and beyond not just for Jerald, but for the entire family. I'd cook elaborate meals with everyone's favorite dishes, clean the entire house and served as a pseudo therapist to his granddaughter. When Jerald and I met, he told me that when I touched him on his shoulder the first night we met, it was the same feeling he had when he held his daughter for the first time. I thought no sweeter words were ever spoken and Jerald had a way with words. He was a master of persuasion, often using tears for emphasis.

Jerald and I were married for three years and together for five. In January 2011, he got a bad cold and went to the doctor because he wasn't feeling well and couldn't shake it. My daughter Tereska was getting married and he couldn't travel to New York with me. When I arrived back from the weekend, he was really tired, his chest was hurting. Still not feeling well, he went back to the doctor and told the doctor to put him in the hospital. They called an ambulance from the doctor's office and when they ran an EKG in the ER, the doctor told us that the test revealed that he had a heart attack and was in kidney failure. Jerald had been a diabetic for close to twenty years. He wasn't in the hospital long, but he told the doctors he didn't want to go on dialysis; he wanted to go home and die. I couldn't believe what he was saying, but accepted his decision and told him to promise me that he'd at least not die on February 7th which was his birthday and also our wedding anniversary. After meeting with the doctor, social worker, and family to tell everyone of his decision, he was set up with hospice. The year prior, we had finally moved into our own place, but thought it would be best to set him up at his daughter's house. Jerald took his last breath shortly after midnight on February 8th. He kept his promise and in the end, I kept my vows to him. I was now a widower for the second time.

Jerald wanted to be cremated and in lieu of a church funeral, we had a celebration of life at a local venue where friends and family gathered in memory of Jerald. He left his car to his eldest nephew and to me, he left medical benefits from the State of Delaware and a percentage of his retirement, which I didn't know until after his death. His two artificial legs couldn't be cremated, so I promptly threw them in the trash. A year after Jerald passed, I moved to New York City for two years to help take care of my second grandson. A new life had come into this world and I also began life anew. One of my friends said she prayed so hard for me when I was married to Jerald. She saw through the facade and never cared for him. From that day forward, I vowed to never get married again and told my daughters that if I ever talked about marrying someone again, to commit me to the insane asylum. To commemorate the promise I made to myself, I wanted to do something significant. On 12/13/2014, I married myself in a small ceremony conducted by my daughter Tereska and witnessed by my two grandsons. I had always put men and their wants and needs first. I was rediscovering, falling in love, and being true to myself. I have a level of peace and happiness that I don't want disturbed in any way.

Now look, I'm not dead yet and still have a lot of life left in me, God willing. I haven't given up on dating and have no shortage of potential suitors at 70 years old, but this time around I'm doing the choosing!

JOAN MARRIES HERSELF: DECEMBER 13, 2014.

# A FAMILY AFFAIR

*This past weekend I went home to DE to
attend the celebration of life service for one
of my cousins. Rest In Peace Khalil.*

*I wanted to be there to support my cousin Ethel,
aunt Sara Jane + the rest of my family. More than
half the sanctuary was filled with family.*

*My mom has always subscribed to the notion that funerals
are more for the living than the person who's departed.
And while we mourn the departed loved one, the moment
is a chance for family and friends to come together, say
their final goodbyes, pay respect, and reflect. I have a
HUGE family and by belonging to both the Haman and
Mitchell families, I'm probably related to half of Delaware.*

*I got a chance to see family, especially some
cousins that I haven't seen in ages and even
met a few new ones. It did my heart good.*

*We celebrate the life of Khalil Mizpah Williams "K
and Huka Buck" as he was affectionately called.*

*In this moment, I'm also celebrating my mom for always
keeping me connected to family and reinforcing the
importance of showing up when it matters the most.*

#celebratelifewithjoan #70DaysofJoan

When my first husband and I separated, we were living in a trailer behind my parents' house. I was working at Dupont and had a monthly car payment of $110 coming directly out of my paycheck because I had gotten a loan from the company's credit union. On top of that, Theodore refused to pay child support. When we went to court, he produced false documents and was only ordered to pay $25 a week. He paid twice and never paid again. I never took him back to court because I was still afraid of him and didn't want to press the matter. As a result, I couldn't pay my bills and filed for bankruptcy. Our trailer was also repossessed. In those days, they published such things and someone told me that they read the notice in the paper. I flat out denied it. If you're reading this, whoever you were, you read it right.

This was around the time I met John. I didn't tell him about my bankruptcy and we left the trailer to move in with him at Iron Hill Apartments in Newark, DE. Tereska was in the second grade and Tanya in the first. It was a convenient transition and no one was the wiser. My debt was erased.

I filed a second time when I was working for IBM. I was in so much debt trying to keep up with a certain lifestyle to show that I had it all together while raising two kids as a single mom. Debt erased again, clean slate. I was embarrassed, but I realized that I had to do what was necessary and required of me at the time for my family.

And that's exactly what I was thinking when my father asked me to sell my house which was located in Overview Gardens in New Castle, DE. We moved there shortly after John passed to give the girls a fresh start. My brother Ham brought Daddy up to our house one day and he asked me to come home to Townsend to take care of my mother who was living with us at the time. A few of my siblings had conspired to move Daddy to a high rise and sell the house and land in Townsend. He didn't want to leave his home and told me that if I sold my house, the house in Townsend would be mine when he and mom passed. When I decided to take daddy up on his offer, there was a rumor that I lost the house, and it spread through the family like wildfire.

Mom lived with us for some time before I made the decision to move back to the house I had grown up in; Townsend was home. Mom was diagnosed with manic depression and had to be placed in a mental hospital at one point. After she was released from the hospital, she went to a group home for a short time, but I decided to bring her home with me. Back then, people didn't talk about mental illness. Mom's manic depression was a sickness that she couldn't control.

JOAN WITH HER GIRLS AND PARENTS AT A FAMILY GATHERING.

A family member said that I was only taking care of mom for personal gain. Other similar comments and innuendos made it a hurtful time and could not have been further from the truth. I remembered how badly she was treated by church members and even family. I uprooted my girls from their friends, schools and lives to move us to rural Delaware. The four of us shared one room, Mom and Daddy had separate rooms, and there was only one bathroom in the house. Who would subject their kids to that for personal gain. My main concern was for Mom's well-being and quality of life. I wanted her to live with dignity, with the type of care and kindness she showered on so many people for years. She lost her mother at a young age and was sent to live with an aunt in New York City while her father moved to Detroit and married another woman. Mom never talked about her younger years, but I can only imagine that the bottled up sadness, anger, and living a life she didn't choose for herself contributed to her mental decline and a nervous breakdown in her 40s.

JOAN'S MOTHER, ESSAMOND MITCHELL.

Mom was diagnosed with early onset Alzheimer's and she was also incontinent. She needed constant monitoring and after a while couldn't be left alone. She'd wander off or get up in the middle of the night to cook something and leave all the burners on while she went back to bed. In 1991, she suffered a massive stroke, which left her paralyzed on one side and without the ability to speak. We could no longer take care of her and had to move her to a nursing home where she held on for another six years.

Everyone thought that Daddy would outlive Mom, even him, but in 1993 he fell in the backyard and broke his hip. After his surgery to fix his hip, he never opened his eyes and said he was talking to his Lord. He was always independent and knew what a broken hip could mean for someone his age. He was 101.

Even though it's been over 30 years and I've forgiven and healed, the sheer level of hate and discord during a time of grief was a pivotal moment for me. My kindness and desire to help was being turned into something ugly and I had no way to defend myself against the barrage of accusations, misperceptions, and attacks on my character. I was the enemy and beside my daughters, I only had one person in my corner. One of the misperceptions and lies that continued to permeate was the belief that my father left me a ton of money. That was far from the truth and I ended up borrowing money to pay for his funeral. I received constant demands from my family to see our father's will. I even received a typewritten letter dated 7/6/93 which I still have to this day. It says...

"Now should have been a time of family coming together, yet just the opposite has and is happening because of some key ingredients that are missing in your character such as trust, honesty, integrity, and open communication.

Many are fooled by your smile and sweet words, you can be very convincing (some things haven't changed since childhood).

I don't hate or dislike you, actually I have a heart full of love for you. I hope and pray that God will step in and break the spirit of deceit and disharmony I see within you.

While you may not like this note, I hope you respect the fact that I am willing to stand up and say what most family members think and feel about you. We are all praying for you. While it has been noted that you moved home to care for our parents, many benefits have also been reaped by you and your family, I don't think anyone begrudges those either. Your efforts have been appreciated."

I don't know why I didn't tear the letter up, but maybe I kept it as proof of what I've gone through and how far I've come. The words cut like a knife and I did in some ways feel like I was being persecuted because of who I was and not those vile, nasty things that were written or said about me.

It was a very dark time. I didn't talk to my siblings for a long time and when I did, I was the one who extended an olive branch. I have forgiven them, but 30 years later, the scars are still there, you just can't see them. Before my eldest sister Mary died, she said she was happy that I was there to take care of Mom and Daddy and thanked me. Maybe she was making amends to ensure that she would get into heaven, but it didn't matter, I knew my heart.

WE ALL GOT RELIGION

We're in the final countdown...10 days before my mom's 70th. The last post will be next Saturday.

Today, I want to pause and take this time to thank each and every person who joined me as a guest contributor. You answered my request and immediately said yes to expressing what it means to celebrate life with my mom.

I won't list each name...but please go back through my posts to read.

To my guest contributors, your kind words and expressions of love and friendship have meant more to my mom than you'll ever know...it means more to her than any gift. You took time out of your busy lives to pay tribute to her in a very public way. She'll always treasure it. A special shout out to those of you who have also commented...so heartwarming.

My mom has lost several of her closest friends over the years and while heartbreaking on so many levels, the one thing that I witnessed first hand between her and those who she lost is that they always expressed how they felt about each other until the very end. There were no words left unspoken.

Ever since I was a little girl, I witnessed the true essence of their love and friendship that withstood the test of time, distance, and the daily rigmarole of life. What a special blessing to celebrate today!

#celebratelifewithjoan #70DaysofJoan

You can't choose your family, but you can choose your friends, and one of my friendships helped shape my thinking on religion and spirituality. I was introduced to a different side of spirituality versus religion through a friend who encouraged me to read books on unity and the power of the subconscious mind.

I do believe that people are placed in your life for a reason, season, or lifetime and this friendship was for a reason and season. One of our interns at IBM introduced me to her mother's friend as I was trying to lose weight and the friend was selling some Dick Gregory diet products. I didn't care, I just wanted to lose weight. I may have lost a few pounds, but gained an instant friend. She would come up with these hare-brained, get rich ideas and I'd be right there with her. We even started a company called A-1 Typing Business, but that didn't last. She and her husband thought that I was so talented and should share my skills with the world.

I grew up being taught to fear God...it was all fire and brimstone. You couldn't dance, couldn't wear pants, had to cover your head and not enjoy life, but sacrifice here on Earth so that you could get your reward in Heaven.

I had drunk the kool-aid at some of the churches I belonged to and saw a lot of things that supposedly went against the teachings of the Bible. People were living double lives, pastors of churches were running with multiple women outside of their wives.

The New Oxford American Dictionary defines religion as "the belief in and worship of a superhuman power or powers, especially a God or gods." It's a very personal thing. Through this friendship, I discovered that God is indeed a spirit and that more importantly, God is love and in everything.

Daddy would always say "take your burden to the Lord and leave it there." Most people who attend church heed the pastor's invitation to come to the altar at some point during the service. There, they are prayed over and told to leave their troubles at the altar, trusting that God will take care of them. It's a metaphor for trusting in God and having faith that He will see you through whatever you're going through and that it's not your load to carry alone. I didn't and still don't understand why people who proclaim to believe in God and trust in the Lord leave the altar and bring their burdens right back with them. I believe in scripture and my favorite one is Proverbs 3:5-6: "Trust in the Lord with all your heart and lean not on your own understanding; in all your ways submit to Him, and He will make your paths straight." Even though I hurt and have experienced tremendous loss, I can celebrate life in the midst of it all because I know this too shall pass. He has my back, front, side, and told me to trust in Him and I do just that every single day.

JOAN WITH DEAR FRIEND, MARGARET WRIGHT.

JOAN'S HOUSE

Someone asked me the other day, "You and your mom have the perfect relationship. Do you ever argue or get upset with each other?!" The person wasn't trying to be mean, but was in true amazement of our relationship.

My response was..."my mom is my best friend. Mother/daughter relationships can be complex, but our relationship isn't perfect but it's pretty perfect for us."

There was a time when we hit a rough patch. I was trying to be grown, grown after I graduated from college and wanted to assert my "independence." Joan wasn't having it AT ALL and let me know point blank. It stung. I won't go into details, but we barely spoke for a few weeks or so. Y'all, it was not good and my little feelings were hurt. I think we both were hurt. We spoke honestly, got over it and mended things. It was very emotional, but communication was key.

Our relationship has evolved and has always been based on love, respect and trust. We don't always agree on things, we get on each other's nerves sometimes but I give her grace because she's the mama. She asks me to do things that I don't want and sometimes I give in and sometimes I'm like please don't ask me to do that, no.

She doesn't butt into my life or weigh in on decisions I make for the most part. She gives her opinion when I ask. We promptly apologize when we're wrong and give each other space when needed. She knows her daughter and I know my Mommy. Some call me little Joan and I take that as a compliment, but my mother never tries to change me or make me into her even though she sometimes lives vicariously through me. Heck, I do the same regarding her.

Yes, we talk every day... the conversation can range from the most mundane like what did you eat for breakfast, laughing about something cray cray to more serious topics like life's biggest mysteries and our dreams. She's one of the funniest and sassiest people I know.

I celebrate her because I know her life and what it's taken for her to get to the place she's in now... the good, the bad and the ugly and some things I probably shouldn't know. She's made countless sacrifices and has always put her girls first.

I know that I am extremely blessed.

So many of my friends don't have relationships with their mothers, biological mothers who were never part of their lives outside of giving birth to them, friends who only talk with their moms a few times a year or have relationships filled with tension, hurt and anger. I see you.

I have friends whose mothers are ill and the relationship has changed to one of caregiver, friends whose mothers have passed...they're missing their mother tremendously as that's a pain and void that never goes away. I see you.

I said in an earlier post that my mom and I won't have any regrets about our relationship when either of us leaves this earth even if it's tomorrow and that's why I celebrate her life today.

#celebratelifewithJoan #70DaysofJoan

If a sitcom were to be written about my life, it would be a drama called Joan's House because my home was always open for someone in need. After all, I was doing my missionary work and my girls were missionaries in training. It actually started with my mother and how she used to help those in need, but where she would give and provide outwardly, I opened up my home to people and made them a part of our family. Mainly women and children who were down on their luck or in bad situations. It was never lost on me what I went through with my first husband and it was my way of giving back. They were always mothers and daughters. I felt a kinship to each of them and willingly shared my home and resources...sometimes having my girls to go without or share their rooms. I didn't ask for anything in return.

To this day, I still do my missionary work in some form or another and it gives me the greatest joy. It's not something I tell people that I do, but it's a way to honor the values that my mother taught me as a young girl and my way of truly living how Christ taught us to be in this world.

I celebrated my 50th birthday on my 47th birthday because I wanted to have a party on a Saturday and when I checked the date for when I'd turn 50, it was a weekday and me being the Leo that I am, I wanted to have a celebration on my actual birthday during the day I wanted.

Forty years after John died, I manifested and said that I was going to Celebrate Life. I coined the phrase, it's my mantra. I remember going to a funeral once and people still do this when they say "we're going to celebrate the life of [Insert Name]." There were so many flowers, people saying all these wonderful things about the deceased. I said to myself, no one's going to celebrate my life AFTER I die, I am celebrating now. In an act of love, I took my daughters to a funeral home when they were teenagers. I assured them that I wasn't sick or dying, but I wanted to make arrangements so that they'd know my wishes before I passed. I didn't want them to stress over what to do when the time came and I wanted them to view death as a natural progression of life and that it's not to be feared.

When I had my two daughters, the only thing I prayed for is to live long enough to be there for them as long as God allowed and I prayed that would be a very long time. I love being a mom and now a grandmother. My kids were my priority and the most important people to me. I could have done certain things differently. I shied away from having deep conversations about life including racism, sex, men, and relationships. It stemmed from how I was raised and certain things were grown folk talk, not for children. Instead they were self-taught, read books, watched TV, and observed life. I tried my best to give them the best life.

I raised Tereska and Tanya differently, but gave them both the same love and nurturing. Tereska and Tanya had vastly different personalities. Tereska is an extrovert and Tanya was an introvert. I dressed them alike until Tereska told me that she didn't want to dress alike anymore and wanted to pick out her own clothes. I did it as a way to make them equals so that Tanya wouldn't get hand-me-downs, but I acquiesced and let them be individuals. I put a lot of pressure on Tereska...pressure that Tanya could not have dealt with at all. For example, if Tereska was sick, I'd still make her go to school, but if Tanya even had so much as the sniffles, I'd make her stay home. Tereska still reminds me of that to this day! Tanya wanted to be a beautician and Tereska wanted to be an artist, but I swayed them away from their dreams. I was ignorant, didn't have the exposure, and wasn't aware of the opportunities for them to explore those career options. I was trying to steer them in the best direction to secure their futures so they wouldn't have to be dependent on a man versus encouraging them to follow their dreams and passions. I did what I thought was best at the time.

TERESKA AND TANYA CELEBRATING THEIR BIRTHDAYS IN NYC.

My proudest moment was when my girls graduated from high school and college. People said that I couldn't raise them on my own and that they'd grow up to be nothing. We proved the naysayers wrong. On the flip side, my most challenging moment was when Tanya graduated and went to college. I got very depressed and felt that I didn't have a purpose anymore, like no one needed me. I had a fleeting thought that there was no use in living. It was a scary thought, but I was able to bring myself out of it.

Just when I thought my most challenging time as a mom was after Tanya graduated, I was caught for a major loop in 2015. Tanya became ill Labor Day weekend. She had a bad headache, was vomiting and initially went to urgent care. What was originally suspected as a viral infection that needed to run its course ended up being a stage 4+ cancer diagnosis. Only days later I rushed her to the ER after she lost all feeling on her right side. After initial testing, she was diagnosed with stage 4 melanoma, the cancer had already spread to her brain...there were 4 large tumors discovered and contributed to bouts of severe seizures. Not my baby, this couldn't be real. The doctor had tears in his eyes when he was delivering the results. When Tanya heard the diagnosis, she started screaming. I was shocked and couldn't believe what I was hearing. I tried my best to stay calm and console her, but completely broke into pieces when I called Tereska who was at work in New York City to tell her the news.

After Tanya came home the first time after she was released from the hospital, she said "I want a church funeral, good singing and good preaching." She accepted that she was going to die and was at peace. I told her that we didn't have to talk about that now and she simply asked me, "well don't you have things planned out for when you die?"

Tanya passed away on December 2, 2015 at the age of 44 after a two-month battle with the disease.

In Tanya's case, it was caught in the last stages and the rounds of chemo and radiation therapy were futile given the aggressive nature of the disease. In the two months after the diagnosis, we set out to do all of the things she loved...spending quality time with De'Andre who had just turned 9 when she passed away, eating at her favorite restaurants, and traveling. She became unresponsive while on a family cruise to the Caribbean over the Thanksgiving holiday and had to be air-lifted back to the States. I flew back to Christiana Medical Center with her and Tereska stayed to keep everyone's spirits up and to celebrate De'Andre's birthday. It was a trip that she had looked forward to for over a year and her last desire was to be able to make the trip with her son and the rest of our family. I had dealt with death before, but it was unnatural for a child to pass away before the parent. Wasn't it?

At the final viewing and inspection, De'Andre told me that he thought it would be best if he went to live with his dad. I lost my baby and in a sense my grand-baby at the same time. The pain was unbearable. If I could have died for her, I would have taken her place. I had to be strong for Tanya and De'Andre and not until we came home from the funeral did I finally break down and cry. I was living by myself for the first time in my entire life. Tanya only cared about what was going to happen to De'Andre and her final wish was for him to live with me and for me to raise him. After he left, De'Andre would call me to come and get him. He was living in a new environment along with his father's girlfriend who didn't want him there. He started to be influenced and hanging around the wrong crowd. I could see the change in him and felt powerless. I filed for emergency custody and took his dad to court, but in the end decided not to fight De'Andre's father. The court did mandate that I was to be made aware of De'Andre's address at all times. I was spiraling and felt like I was losing my mind. The grief was too much.

Soon after Tanya's funeral, Tereska called and said she wanted to start a nonprofit called the Brown Skin Too Foundation (aka Brown Skin, Too) to honor Tanya and educate others about melanoma in people of color. She wanted my help and I immediately said yes. It was a way to deal with the grief and channel my sadness into helping other people. And so the healing began.

"How are you going to celebrate life now?" Remember this is the harsh comment that I mentioned from a well-meaning friend in the beginning. Tanya would have wanted me to do it, and I became even more determined to celebrate my life. And I did. I traveled, celebrated my 65th birthday in grand style, worked when I wanted to, visited with friends and family, dated a few gentlemen...hey, I said I wasn't dead. Still married to myself.

JOAN GETTING HER FIRST TATTOO AT 70.

WORKING GIRL

TAKEOVER THURSDAY

Today's guest post courtesy of Patricia Gordon McMichael

I am so fortunate to call Joan my friend. We met way back when we both worked for Advanta. I always received a wonderful smile whenever I spoke with Joan and she never failed to ask "How can I help you?" When the company was bought out, and we were going through so much change, Joan remained upbeat and positive. Unfortunately, Joan was one of the many people let go during the transition. As fate would have it, our paths crossed again several years later at a Relay for Life, where I learned the heartbreaking news of her daughter Tanya's passing. I was awed by how Joan painfully accepted her fate and was using it to educate and help others. Such strength!

Thankfully since that meeting we have stayed in touch. We meet for lunch when we can and we pick up right where we were the last time we met. I have had the pleasure of meeting several of Joan's wonderful family members at our lunches and I have so enjoyed their company.

I cannot begin to tell of all the ways this wonderful woman has inspired me - The work she has done to spread the word on the danger of skin cancer to people of color. Working to create a scholarship in her daughter Tanya's name. The great closeness she has with her sisters, grandchildren and daughter Tereska are to be admired. Starting a second career teaching children (I bet she is an awesome teacher!). Her videos full of inspirational tidbits that she creates during her early morning walks. Her wonderful smile! Her faith in the

> good of others and that things will always work out. Her strength in never letting life's hard times keep her down. And her daily creed to "Celebrate Life!" I try to follow her lead to find and Celebrate Life every day, which has made me a better person and improved my life.
>
> As I mentioned - I am so fortunate to call Joan my friend!
>
> —Tricia

I've worked to earn money ever since I was a young girl and while I've held various jobs from a retail store employee to being a substitute teacher. I wouldn't necessarily call my employment tenure a career, which is defined as "an occupation undertaken for a significant period of a person's life and with opportunities for progress." I spent over twenty years working as an executive assistant for various companies such as IBM, Bank of America, DuPont, American Express Centurion Bank. I was good at my job—actually, better than good. I always held myself and others to a standard of excellence and to this day, I count many of my former managers as dear friends and have fond memories of when companies really did treat their employees as family. I always tell everyone that I'm going to expire and not retire.

I enjoy being around people, keeping busy and of course keeping some change in my pocket to feed my zest for travel. My primary goal for years wasn't about climbing the corporate ladder, although I had plenty of opportunities, but it was about being present and taking care of my girls. I struggled as a single mom and made many sacrifices for years.

When I die, there will be no funeral. I've often said this and people don't believe me. I don't envision a long obituary listing my work history or career accomplishments. At the end of your life, that won't really matter. It's a well known saying that no one on their deathbed says, "I wish I'd spent more time at work."

JOAN AT THE IBM OFFICE IN WILMINGTON, DE.

The one thing I know to be true is how so many wonderful people entered my life throughout my career journey. At just six, I set out to be a missionary...to help people and make a difference. All of those work experiences guided me on that path. They shaped me and expanded my outlook on people and the world. There are too many people to name and I would inadvertently leave someone off the list if I even started, but those who have touched my life, whether it's been in a small or significant way, know who they are and what they mean to me. I believe in the old adage of giving people their flowers while they can smell them and I have been a direct recipient of that kindness as well.

From managers who took a chance on a single mom and were vested in my girls' success as much as they were in mine, to former coworkers who've become life-long friends, and friends who I've held in confidence through many of our shared experiences, there are no words to express my level of gratitude for your steadfast devotion and commitment to our bond. I have dear friends who have passed on, but have left an imprint on my heart and continue to be a source of inspiration through how they lived their lives. I will make one exception...my dear friend Jean Garner who I met when we both worked for IBM. We were friends for 50 years before she passed away. While she lived in California, we talked every day. She used to always tell me how special and smart I was...she saw in me what I didn't see in myself. She was tough, confident and cursed like a sailor, but she had a heart of gold. I still have the letters that she used to write me.

But, it wasn't always roses and sunshine. I've had some awful bosses and coworkers who tried to break my soul and take away my shine. In those instances I stayed true to myself and never let them see me sweat. I sure did get the hell out of those jobs quickly, sometimes without a safety net. God always made a way.

DAILY MEDICINE

CELEBRATING LIFE IS MY RELIGION

My mom LOVES nature and the outdoors...anything related to nature, she's like a little kid discovering for the first time. I get excited seeing her so full of joy. Literally everything from a new moon, rainbow, the first snow of the season, the ocean, flowers blooming, and so much more.

Funny story, a few weeks ago there was a Strawberry Moon (not its actual color), but it's June's full moon. Grayson and I were coming home and saw it bright in the sky...it was absolutely breathtaking. I immediately called my mom to tell her about it. She was already in bed, but was so excited, she got up, rushed out of the house in her night clothes and went to see for herself.

I won't tell you the shenanigans that ensued in her pursuit to see, but it involved a New Castle County police officer, a cell phone, video evidence and a moment more memorable than seeing the Strawberry Moon! I can't remember the last time I laughed so hard.

Here's to celebrating the beauty of nature and its many splendid wonders.

#celebratelifewithjoan #70DaysofJoan

Outside of my girls and grandchildren, the things I love the most are butterflies, walking outside, dancing, and taking pictures... sometimes I get to experience them all at the same time. Those are extra special days and luckily for me, they happen often. I love looking at the pictures I've taken and reflecting on that moment in time of the people, places and things that I've captured. Pictures tell stories and the fact that I've been able to take so many brings me tons of joy especially when I'm asked by family and friends if I have a picture that they recall I took of them. I know it's a gift that they'll always treasure, especially if it's of a loved one who's no longer here.

Growing up as a country girl, being outdoors was always special to me. I fell in love with nature...from seeing the sun peeking out across the horizon at daybreak, catching the first flakes from a fresh snowfall, leaves drifting to the ground in the fall, to the liquid sunshine that April showers bring, it's all magical to me.

During the start of the COVID-19 pandemic, I started a YouTube channel called Inspirational Walks with Joan, which combined my daily walking routine with imparting words of wisdom. It's something that I shared privately with friends and family for years and still do to this day.

Walking is daily medicine for me. It makes me happy, gives me serenity, and helps me put things into perspective. The mental clarity it provides has helped me make some major life decisions. In my mind, the endorphins I get from walking give me a high that surpasses any pill or drug.

Although I'm now able to walk up to three miles a day, sometimes more, it hasn't always been a walk in the park (get it?! LOL!). There was a time where I couldn't walk half a mile.

I was a runner in my early 30s. My husband John and I would get up early in the morning to run before work, and I'd also run during my lunch break. I loved running and thought I could pick right back up with a little help in my 50s when I began training for the Virginia Beach Rock and Roll Half Marathon. I started experiencing pain in my right knee. My trainer told me I probably needed new running shoes. Well that was a hundred dollars wasted. A trip to an orthopedist confirmed that I had arthritis in my knee. I ended up walking the half marathon and the knee pain persisted.

JOAN ON HER DAILY WALKS.

As the years progressed, my knee pain got worse and spread to both knees. My doctor suggested that I have knee replacement surgery, which I was strongly against and ignored his suggestion. I'm so happy I did because if I went ahead with the surgery I would not have found an even better solution for me and that is walking.

My daughter Tereska planned a 50th birthday trip to Morocco. The itinerary was fast-paced and included an intense amount of walking over various surfaces throughout the tour of four cities. We were concerned if I'd be able to keep up or even go, but I was determined to celebrate with my daughter and the thirty guests who were also embarking on this adventure with us.

The walking and pace during the trip ended up being an elixir for my arthritis. I walk daily because it truly is my medicine and cured me of my arthritis pain. Of course, I'm no doctor, but I can tout the benefits of moving my body daily. Dedication, commitment, and consistency are the key for me.

DIDN'T SEE THAT COMING

*When my mom departs her earthly body, there
will be no formal funeral or celebration of life.*

*This is something that we discussed YEARS ago. I have
my instructions and she remains very adamant. Lord,
if I have a funeral she will come back to haunt me.*

*She wanted to make it clear NOW, outside of the
emotional impact, sadness and overwhelming grief and
stress that one feels when they lose a loved one.*

*There's also the sobering reality that she may outlive
me...we've experienced Tanya's passing but it's not
something we focus on. We focus on living life TODAY.*

*The estate planning is complete...will, durable power
of attorney, healthcare proxy, life insurance, etc.*

*No one knows the day, minute or hour of our
death...only God knows. That's why she can
and chooses to celebrate her life now.*

How are you choosing to celebrate life today?

#celebratelifewithjoan #70DaysofJoan

With Tanya gone and De'Andre with his dad, I decided to move to Massachusetts in 2017 with Tereska, her husband, and my grandson while they settled in. They moved from Northern New Jersey to Massachusetts for her husband's new job. My grandson was starting kindergarten and Tereska had taken a new job with a marketing firm in Boston. I made some new friends, traveled, and spent a lot of time with my G-baby. It was like old times from when we were in New York City when he was born. After Tanya passed,

Tereska started a not-for-profit in her memory called Brown Skin Too Foundation to provide education and awareness of melanoma and promote skin wellness among people of color. We were busy with the work of the foundation and I kept myself occupied. After a year, in 2018, I decided to move back to Delaware and start a new chapter in my life.

Here I go again telling someone how to live their life. When will I learn?

My third husband Tyrone and I were still friends until his passing. In July 2018, I asked him if he had ever done a colonoscopy. He was having some health issues and I was going to the doctor with him to try and figure out what was going on. He said he never had a colonoscopy and boy when he told me that, I started preaching that I couldn't believe he'd never had one and how important it was to get. I called to make the appointment for him and the nurse asked me "well, when was the last time you had one?" I just knew I was up to date and called the place where I received it, but they had gone out of business. I called my primary care physician and they had no records. I was adamant that I'd had at least two. I scheduled my colonoscopy on August 8, 2018. Just routine, I was perfectly healthy. I ate right, exercised, and didn't abuse alcohol or drugs. I took care of myself.

When I went for my colonoscopy, Tyrone came with me as I was prohibited from driving myself home after the procedure. When I awoke from the procedure, Tyrone was sitting next to me waiting for me to wake up. The gastroenterologist came in to tell me the results. I didn't have a shadow of doubt in my mind that I passed with flying colors, but to my surprise, I got the news that no one expects or wants to hear. You have cancer. I thought I heard wrong and was sure they made a mistake. The doctor told me that I had to have surgery right away and referred me to an oncologist. I didn't have any symptoms and my bowels were regular. Not me, I thought. I remained calm, but Tyrone became very emotional and started crying. It wasn't what I needed at that moment, but I understood his concern. I didn't call my daughter Tereska until after I got home. She was subdued, but I could tell she was worried. After all, her father had passed away of colon cancer years prior. I told the oncologists that I couldn't schedule the surgery as we were going on vacation. I had my daughter and two G-babies with me and we were going to California. I was in denial like nothing was wrong. Nothing to see here folks.

I decided to have the surgery on September 28th and made sure I was listed as a ghost patient so no one got wind of my being in the hospital. The same day, Tereska would be in Delaware to be honored for her work with Brown Skin Too Foundation. It was a black tie affair so in addition to being there for my surgery, she also went to get her hair and makeup done. I insisted and told her to attend the event, tell everyone that I wasn't feeling well, and that she could come back to the hospital afterwards since I'd just be getting out of surgery. I told her to promise that she'd have balloons in my hospital room when I came out of recovery. Tereska got dressed in the hospital bathroom and didn't miss a beat. As the anesthesia was kicking in, I could hear my song "Celebrate" by Kool & The Gang being played over the speakers. My request to the surgery team. The surgery was a success, but I was officially diagnosed with stage 2 colon cancer. They removed 28 lymph nodes and I was in the hospital for 10 days.

During my recovery, I lost 20 pounds, as I had no appetite. Since Tyrone was in the room after I had my colonoscopy and heard the news from my doctor at the same time I did, I swore him to secrecy, but he told his daughter Tylisa. She sent me a frantic text saying that he told her. He apologized and said he was nervous, upset, and didn't know what to do. I asked him to immediately tell her that it was a mistake and that he'd heard wrong. I was furious! I didn't want anyone else to know because if people heard, they would have immediately given me a death sentence. I didn't need any negative energy. I only wanted to focus on living and celebrating life. That was the only thing on my mind.

Earlier that year on Mother's Day, Tereska surprised me with a trip to London, but the trip wasn't until the Thanksgiving holiday. She was taking me to see the Tina Turner Musical before it was announced that it would travel to the U.S. I was deeply touched as this was also a thank you gift from Tereska for me making the sacrifice to come to Massachusetts to help with my grandson. Only two months after my surgery, we were headed on our big adventure, but what Tereska didn't know at the time was that I was still in tremendous pain and my scar tissue was still healing. It was unbearable to walk even a short distance and I was frustrated because Tereska was walking so fast. At one point, I even lost sight of her during one of our evening outings. I didn't want to ruin our trip, so I suffered in pain. Instead I took deep breaths, stayed patient, did my best to stay at peace and focused on everything working out in the end. Of course it did and I am thankful that I didn't do irreparable damage.

In 2019 I got another CT scan and get a blood test every six months. My oncologist said that if I had waited one more year it would have been too late. I'm not yet declared cancer free and since my initial diagnosis I've shared with a few people who only continue to inspire me and focus on the positive. When someone mentions the "C" word aka Cancer, thoughts automatically go to the person dying and is usually followed by negative connotations about the disease. It's a word that I rarely use.

Walking became even more important to me after my surgery. It was part of my recovery. Laying in bed was not an option for me. I went to the park one day for a walk and I overheard two women who were on bikes making fun of me and talking about how slow I was going. I could hardly walk, but I was moving and it was all that mattered. When our paths crossed again, I told them that they shouldn't judge people because you never know what someone is going through. I didn't give an explanation and said my piece.

People always say that I'm so positive and happy in the midst of... well, life.

I make a conscious effort to do so and don't look back on my life with regrets. I'm still here and I want to be my own best friend. That's where I am right now. I don't have time for the small stuff. There have been points in time where celebrating life became a necessity for my survival and my colon cancer diagnosis was a pivotal moment in my kicking it up a notch. Those words from my oncologist, "if I had waited one more year it would have been too late", were not a death sentence to me, but a rallying cry to celebrate my life even more, and I've done so from that day forward. You see my glory, but now you know my story, and it's still being written.

THE END

JOAN AND TERESKA ON MARTHA'S VINEYARD FOR JOAN'S 70TH BIRTHDAY PHOTOSHOOT.

AFTERWORD

Celebrating Life has been my motto for many years. I find something every day to enjoy and be happy about. It might be just looking up at the sky, enjoying the snowflakes, watching the flowers grow, seeing the little kids play, walking on the beach...the list goes on and on.

Over 20 years ago, Tereska gave me a purple journal and told me to start writing my life's story. I jotted a few things down from time to time, but never kept it up. It has always been my dream that my story be told. As you know, I asked my daughter Tereska many times to write my book. On my 70th birthday, she presented me with the gift of agreeing to honor my wish! I am grateful for Tereska taking the time to write my story before I make my transition. I am deeply touched by all the time and energy she has put into this book. We have a special bond and I'm so thankful for such a wonderful daughter. I love her dearly!

During the pandemic I had a lot of time to reminisce about my life and was very anxious to share it with the world. I was no longer afraid to tell the story in my own words and for you to read it firsthand from me and no one else. I've tried to be as authentic as possible. For many years I was ashamed of my life and didn't want to share many parts of it. Whenever I would start trying to write my story, it was very painful because it opened many old wounds that I had tried to suppress. The fear of what others would think of me is gone. Telling my story has been very liberating and has set me free. Remember...the truth shall set you free!

I have many people tell me throughout my life that you are always happy and smiling. It seems like you don't have a care or problem in the world. You are always positive and don't seem to worry about anything. I would answer by saying everyone has something they are going through but it's what you do with it! I clearly remember my Daddy always telling me, "Take your burdens to the Lord and leave them there. That's what I've tried to do most of my adult life. I wanted this book to be written to inspire and encourage those with no hope to believe in themselves, have faith, and to trust in a greater power— whether you call it God, Jehovah, Buddha, or the Universe. Just believe.

When I experienced the death of my second husband John, an older lady friend called and said to read Philippians 4:13, which says "I can do all things through Christ which strengtheneth me." I have used that scripture over and over in my lifetime.

Many have been inspired by my positive, upbeat mentality, and my commitment to living my motto of "Celebrate Life". I also believe happiness is a choice. I now make conscious choices for my happiness as I continue to enjoy each day and celebrate my life. And while this book recounts only my first 70 years, there has been so much that has happened since 2022 when Tereska and I set out on this journey. All in all, I have continued to live up to my motto. Now go celebrate life, too!

—Joan

ABOUT THE AUTHOR

Tereska E. James has always had a passion for writing ever since she won a school-wide award in the 4th grade for a play that she wrote focused on her family and served as a "ghost writer" in the 5th grade by penning Mother's Day greetings for her classmates after she was selected to read the one she did for her mother in front of the class. By day, Tereska is a marketing and advertising executive with more than 20 years in agency client services. She is a member of Alpha Kappa Alpha Sorority, Inc. and Jack and Jill of America, Inc. and also the past president of Brown Skin Too Foundation, which she founded after the loss of her sister to melanoma.

Prior to her mother's memoir, Tereska also wrote and self-published a motivational guide called "Single-licious: For a Lifetime or the In-Between Time" in 2009, which touted all of the things a woman could do during the "single" season. She often contributes her writing skills and talents for personal, philanthropic, and business pursuits.

Tereska, born and raised in Delaware, received her undergraduate degree from the University of Delaware and currently resides in the greater Boston area.